GUERILLA FURNITURE DESIGN

How to Build Lean, Modern Furniture with Salvaged Materials

WILL HOLMAN

Photography by Kip Dawkins

Storey Publishing

The mission of Storey Publishing is to serve our customers by publishing practical information that encourages personal independence in harmony with the environment.

Edited by Philip Schmidt and Sarah Guare
Art direction by Alethea Morrison
Book design by Kelley Galbreath
Photo styling by Neely Dykshorn
Indexed by Christine R. Lindemer, Boston Road Communications

Cover and interior photography by © Kip Dawkins Photography, except © Alfonso Elia, 2;
   © Daniel Wicke, 3; © Ryan LeCluyse, 100, 103, and 179 (second row, far right)
Illustrations by © Koren Shadmi

Storey Publishing
210 MASS MoCA Way
North Adams, MA 01247
www.storey.com

Printed in China by R.R. Donnelley
10 9 8 7 6 5 4 3 2 1

Library of Congress Cataloging-in-Publication Data

Holman, Will.
   Guerilla furniture design : how to build lean, modern furniture with
   salvaged materials / by Will Holman.
      pages cm
   Includes index.
   ISBN 978-1-61212-303-5 (pbk. : alk. paper)
   ISBN 978-1-61212-304-2 (ebook)   1.   Lean manufacturing—Management.
   2.   Furniture industry and trade.   I. Title.
HD58.9.H653 2015
684.1—dc23
                                        2014033718

CONTENTS

"
THIS 'COUNT
REVELATION
OR REDUNDA
PRESENT SO
THAT ONE CA
OFF THE WAS
AFFLUENT M

CHARLES JENCKS

ER-CULTURE'
OF SLACK
NCY IN OUR
IETY PROVES
N LIVE
TE OF AN
AJORITY."

ACKNOWLEDGMENTS

I want to thank Amanda, for putting up with Saturdays in the shop, sawdust in the living room, and life with a guerilla. You are my first reader, my best design critic, my inspiration, and my support.

Thank you to my parents, Fran and John, for supporting my education, teaching me responsibility, instilling a solid Protestant work ethic, and selling me that Corolla for a comically good price. Thank you especially to my mother for her persistent lessons in grammar, however fitfully they may have been absorbed.

Thanks to my siblings and siblings-in-law (Spence, Ellie, Sara, James, and Jane) for their encouragement, legal assistance, design help, copyediting, material donations, and absorption of various discarded furniture prototypes over the years.

Thanks to the fine editors, designers, and staff at Storey Publishing for believing in my story and making this book a reality. Thanks also to Kip Dawkins and his assistant Marcie for the beautiful photographs, and to Kelley Galbreath for designing the book. A special thanks to Philip Schmidt, who first contacted me to feature one of my designs in his book, *PlyDesign,* and went on to e-mail editors on my behalf and to edit this book for clarity, content, and coherence.

And last, thank you to all the teachers I have had over the years. They taught me about writing, aesthetics, art, architecture, design, carpentry, and ethics. In chronological order: William Jones, Juan Castro, Albert Knight, Robert Goll, Salahuddin Choudhury, Timothy Castine, Hunter Pittman, Christopher Pritchett, Eugene Egger, Paolo Soleri, David Tollas, Mark Melonas, Seth Scott, Andrew Freear, Daniel Wicke, Johnny Parker, Steven Long, John Marusich, Sara Williamson, Cynthia Main, Blake Sloane, John Preus, Tadd Cowen, and Theaster Gates Jr.

GUERILLA D
IS A SET OF 7
FOR BUILDIN
MODERN FU
OUT OF SALV
MATERIALS

ESIGN
ACTICS
IG LEAN,
RNITURE
AGED

U.S. ARMY FIELD MANUALS are handbooks for military personnel, published by the Department of Defense. Since World War II, hundreds of titles have been published, including civilian-friendly topics like first aid and wilderness survival. Each manual breaks down complex concepts into manageable pieces, illustrated with simple black-and-white diagrams.

THE TERM *GUERILLA* — Spanish for "little war" – was invented in the early nineteenth century. In modern usage, guerilla describes both insurrectionary warfare and insurgent fighters themselves. Such fighters are tough, resourceful, and adept at living off the land.

GUERILLA DESIGN, as described in this manual, is a set of tactics for building lean, modern furniture out of salvaged materials. These techniques are explained generally and then illustrated with a series of case studies, sorted by material: paper, wood, plastic, and metal. Each project is presented in detail, with the assumption that materials and methods will be adapted to conditions in the field.

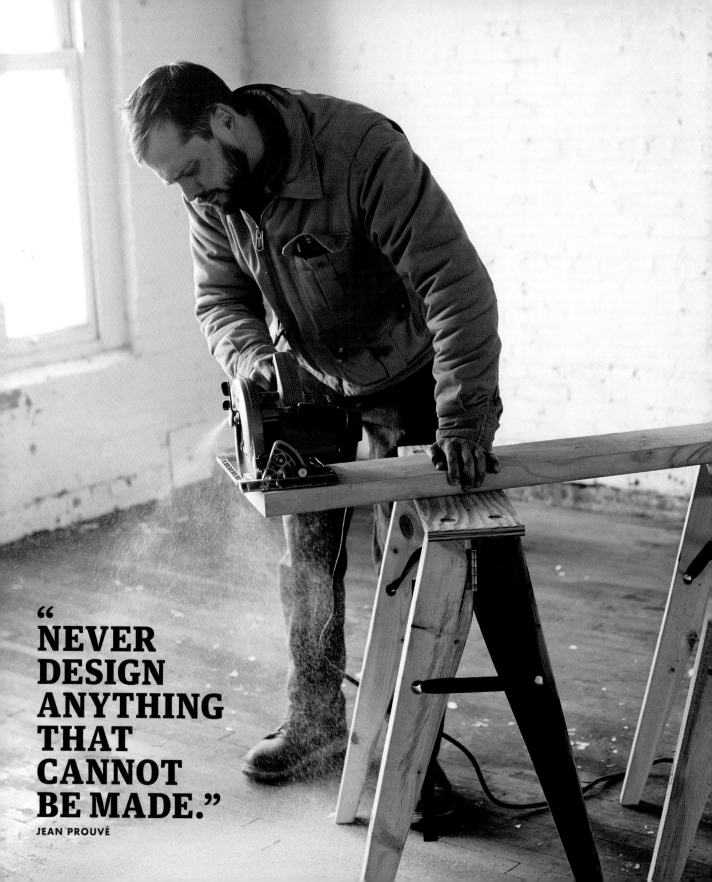

"NEVER DESIGN ANYTHING THAT CANNOT BE MADE."

JEAN PROUVÉ

THE EDUCATION OF A GUERILLA

I graduated with a degree in architecture from Virginia Tech in May 2007. In June, I packed a van, moved home, and spent a restless summer unsuccessfully searching for work in Baltimore. In August, I put a backpack in the backseat of my '98 Corolla and drove west. I arrived in Cordes Junction, Arizona, one week later.

For the next year I lived at Arcosanti, an experimental community an hour north of Phoenix. Founded in 1970 by Italian architect Paolo Soleri, Arcosanti is a prototype *arcology*, a dense urban system designed to produce its own food and energy. Eager to learn, I worked in the construction department, welding and pouring concrete, expanding the city. The wide-open country was gorgeous, the people warm and welcoming. I spent my Saturdays rooting around Arco's boneyard, home to 40 years' worth of construction debris, scrap metal, scaffolding, and old cars. Dragging fragments back to the workshop, I welded pieces together to create furniture for my co-op apartment.

In the summer of 2008 I headed back to Baltimore, straight into the nascent headwinds of the Great Recession. I spent the next year working at a custom cabinetry shop. At night, I sent out résumés and designed my own projects, hoping the economy would rebound. Architecture firms were devastated by the housing collapse, work was slow, and nobody was hiring. I put aside my architectural dreams for a time and concentrated on developing my woodworking skills, tutored by the master craftsmen at my job.

In the spring of 2009 I applied to the Rural Studio. Founded in 1991 by Auburn University professors Samuel Mockbee and D. K. Ruth, the Rural Studio is an architectural design-build laboratory in Hale County, Alabama. I was accepted into their Outreach program, figuring I could wait out the recession for one more year. The studio was (and still is) engaged in a long-term research project — the 20K House — meant to address the lack of decent low-income housing in the rural South. After eight months at the drafting board, my teammates and I built

FIRST SIGN This is my first attempt at road sign furniture, at Arcosanti.

▼

the ninth 20K House in about 50 days. Our client moved in at the end of June and parked himself on the porch, sitting in a rocking chair I made out of construction scraps.

School over, I looked for jobs across the South — in New Orleans and Birmingham — and back in Baltimore. Nothing came. I managed to rustle up some renovation work around the small town of Greensboro, Alabama, where I was living, spending weeks scraping and repainting the old tin roof on an antebellum home. In late summer I got a job with YouthBuild, a local nonprofit that taught trade skills to young folks (coupled with GED classes) and paid them a small stipend for doing work around the community. That year we built a big vegetable garden, bordered by a fence made of old road signs from the county dump. On the weekends I tinkered with bending extra signs into chairs.

YouthBuild's grant was cut in June 2011. I was out of work and in the wind, again. This time, I pointed the Corolla north, to Chicago, with a tiny U-Haul in tow. But salaried jobs were hard to come by, even in the big city, so I patched together a freelance career — building furniture, writing articles about woodworking, teaching design to teenagers, and working for an artist renovating a group of derelict buildings on the South Side. Many of my friends, co-workers, and former classmates were in the same boat, hustling in a gig economy where steady work seemed increasingly difficult to find.

I recently moved again, halfway back across the country, to my sixth apartment in as many years. This time, work and life conspired to land me back in my hometown. Baltimore — like Chicago, Cleveland, Detroit, or St. Louis — is a rust belt town, scarred by violence, corruption, factory closings, and population loss. Battered as it may be, Baltimore is unbroken, populated with

scrappy artists and makers who are experts at living on the margins. I've taken on a fellowship at a local nonprofit working to develop space for artists in the Station North district. We are leveraging cheap real estate and ubiquitous media into a new culture of making, reimagining our industrial heritage with modern tools.

My design sense was shaped by nomadism, recessionary economics, and the great abundance of America's waste stream. Over the years, it would have been easy to furnish my varied apartments with thrift-store finds and big-box buys. Instead, I looked at each move as a fresh start, a new opportunity to solve a set of old problems: how to get me, and my stuff, off the floor. With little money, few tools, and improvised workshops, I shaped my environment out of paper, plastic, wood, and metal. *Guerilla Furniture Design* is meant to help you do the same.

"YOU HAVE TO FIND YOUR WORLD OF ARCHITECTURE."

SALAHUDDIN CHOUDHURY

▲
20K HOUSE MacArthur Coach sits on the porch of his 20K House in Faunsdale, Alabama.

GUERILLA HISTORY

Guerilla design — grassroots, sustainable, handcrafted — is not a product of just the last few years. While the recession and environmental concerns have driven a recent resurgence in DIY culture, the seeds of self-reliance are deeply rooted in American history.

Native The American continent was first inhabited by a vast array of native peoples. Some were roaming hunter-gatherers and others city-building agrarians, but all were engaged in sophisticated resource management. They extracted all of their food, medicine, and shelter from their environment without depleting the land. Once the horse was introduced, Plains tribes became masterful nomads, following herds of bison and seasonal water sources over thousands of miles.

Colonial In the period leading up to the American Revolution, colonists imported manufactured goods from Europe and exported cash crops like tobacco and timber. This trade reinforced England's economic dominance over the colonies while providing Britons with much-needed lumber. Once the Revolution started, American rebels re-evaluated their dependency on English goods, choosing to make their own furniture, housewares, and clothes — craft as a form of political protest.

Shaker In the mid-nineteenth century, religious fervor swept the country as part of the Great Awakening. Sects splintered off from established churches, and messianic cells sprung up around the country. The Shakers were founded in England in 1747, reaching full strength in America a century later with established communities from New York to Kentucky. Committed to celibacy and ecstatic worship (thus the "shaking"), they supported themselves through the production of furniture and other goods in the belief that work was a form of devotion. The Shakers eventually died out (that whole celibacy thing) but their elegant, minimal furniture has influenced generations of designers.

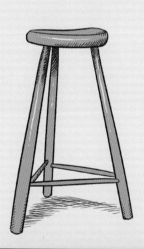

NATIVE The tipi is a brilliant design: a structurally stable, wind-resistant shape wrapped in an insulated tensile membrane — a self-contained dwelling that can be taken down or set up in a few hours.

COLONIAL While typically rustic, early American furniture demonstrates sophisticated knowledge of wood species and joinery techniques. Metal fasteners were expensive, so pioneers used notches, pegs, and wedges instead.

SHAKER Shaker chairs relied on drill-and-peg joinery, executed in common hardwoods. Utilitarian pieces often were made of cheap poplar and finished with milk paint. A hundred years before the Modernists, Shaker craftsmen were working with common materials and simple joinery to produce spare, refined furniture.

Craftsman After the industrial revolution, Americans left the countryside and moved to cities. A certain level of manual competency, once ingrained in the average farm boy, was forgotten on the factory floor. These trends were worrisome to writer and publisher Elbert Hubbard who, in 1895, established a community in East Aurora, New York, devoted to the production of handcrafted furniture, books, clothes, and housewares. Adherents called themselves Roycrofters, after an antiquarian term for craftsman.

Modernist Artist Louise Brigham published *Box Furniture* in 1909. This manual for making furniture out of packing crates was startlingly prescient and full of modern ideas – modularity, recyclability, and material efficiency. Brigham had a rough-edged aesthetic based on cubic forms and common hardware. The pieces used bypass framing, which eliminates joinery by simply running adjoining pieces past one another and fastening at the intersection. Modernist architect Gerrit Rietveld expanded upon Brigham's ideas in his Red Blue chair (1923) and Zig-Zag chair (1934), exchanging traditional techniques for straight cuts, mechanical fasteners, and painted finishes. Forty years later,

architecture professor Ken Isaacs pushed the same ideas further with an "Erector set" system of wood bars and machine bolts that could be assembled into a variety of structures.

Postwar After World War II, the accelerated growth and prosperity of 1950s America were followed by the social tumult of the 1960s and economic stagnation in the 1970s. Designers were quick to react. In 1968, Stewart Brand published the first *Whole Earth Catalog*, a sourcebook of "tools" for homesteading and associated skills. Architect Paolo Soleri founded Arcosanti in the Arizona desert in 1970. Buckminster Fuller developed the geodesic dome as cheap, sustainable housing for the masses. Lloyd Kahn published *Domebook 1 & 2* (1971) and *Shelter* (1973), introducing alternative building methods adapted from both modern designers and indigenous cultures. Victor Papanek and James Hennessey authored the first *Nomadic Furniture* (1973), a guide to DIY flat-pack, inflatable, and disposable furniture. Around that same time, Italian designer Enzo Mari published *Autoprogettazione*, a DIY furniture manual based on standard sizes of milled lumber fastened with simple nails.

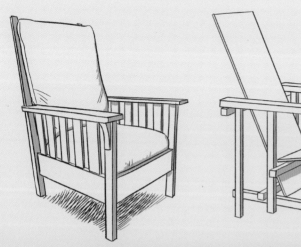

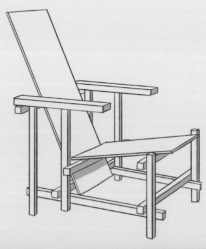

CRAFTSMAN Roycroft furniture patterns featured right angles and lap joinery. The design sense of the Roycrofters influenced Frank Lloyd Wright, Gustav Stickley, and the Arts and Crafts style of the early twentieth century.

MODERNIST Gerrit Rietveld abstracted furniture, reducing it to a simple cloud of parts attached with mechanical fasteners. He did the same in architecture, experimenting with modularity and prefabrication.

POSTWAR The 1960s and '70s saw the launch of many design projects with counterculture intentions. Enzo Mari's chair – named simply "Seat" – was an attempt to radically change the way furniture was designed, distributed, and built.

Punk As the seventies progressed, young folks faced a broken economy and political turmoil. In 1976, The Ramones released their self-titled debut, soon followed by the Sex Pistols' seminal single "Anarchy in the U.K." When their music was banned from commercial radio, the Pistols went DIY, making and distributing homemade tapes on tiny mail-order music labels. The same spirit of self-reliance inspired fashion and graphic design, as punks outfitted themselves in found outfits and advertised their shows with collaged, photocopied posters.

Maker The relative peace and prosperity of the nineties were shattered by the attacks of September 11. Concerns about war, rising energy prices, and the collapse of an Internet-stock bubble damaged the economy. The following decade has seen a resurgence in handmade culture – as a way of saving money, in a search for authenticity, as a reaction against Internet-centric society, or perhaps in a quest for control over something in an increasingly out-of-control world. In 2002, Shoshana Berger and Grace Hawthorne launched *ReadyMade* magazine out of Berkeley, California, showcasing clever furniture designs executed with found objects and off-the-shelf parts. In January 2005, *MAKE* magazine began publication, chronicling the emergent maker community with quarterly issues and an extensive website. Instructables launched that same year as a platform for sharing DIY instructions, quickly followed by Etsy, an online marketplace for handmade goods.

The waves of guerilla design historically have coincided with periods of social and economic upheaval, and today is no different. The Great Recession, climate change, technological innovation, political instability – the world is realigning, and there are more sophisticated resources available to the guerilla than ever before. Makerspaces are sprouting all over, giving ordinary folks access to industrial machinery and expert tutelage (see Makerspaces on page 10). New websites are spreading open-source software and instructions for making just about anything. Urban gardeners are bringing food production back to the cities. Deconstruction and salvage warehouses are mining old buildings for raw materials. Manufacturing is returning to American shores. All of these converging trends have created unprecedented opportunity for the nimble, underground designer: the guerilla.

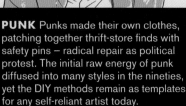

PUNK Punks made their own clothes, patching together thrift-store finds with safety pins – radical repair as political protest. The initial raw energy of punk diffused into many styles in the nineties, yet the DIY methods remain as templates for any self-reliant artist today.

MAKER Concerns about global warming have informed design, from fuel-efficient jetliners and hybrid cars to modular housing and vertical farming. Not coincidentally, today's DIYers are propelled by very old motivations – saving money, getting healthier, and reconnecting with the world.

GUERILLA SUSTAINABILITY

The American continent has been logged, mined, and hunted from coast to coast. Yet, even as settlers were busy cutting forests and plowing up prairie, they were frugal, well aware of the amount of labor it took to make things. We have long been a nation of sock-darners and candle-savers, feeding table scraps to the pigs and boiling bones for soup stock.

In the last century, "green" concepts have come and gone. Citizens were encouraged to economize during the world wars. Rationing saved key resources for the troops overseas. In the 1970s, back-to-the-landers abandoned the suburbs and made a go at organic farming and communal living. Now, it seems like everyone is looking at their carbon footprint and trying a locavore diet. There is legitimate and growing global concern about carbon emissions, peak oil, and a warming planet.

Our culture tends toward reactive, technological solutions to these problems. Proposals abound — building seawalls, pumping carbon emissions underground, driving hybrid cars — all designed to allow us to continue our current lifestyle while somehow mitigating its impact. But these ideas ignore reality: Americans comprise 5 percent of the world population and use 25 percent of the world's energy. There is no easy way out of that equation, only the obvious: we must use *less*.

Frugality is the cornerstone of guerilla sustainability. Most of the projects in this book start with salvaged materials, which are abundant and free. Using alley finds keeps things out of the waste stream. Conventional recycling, while laudable, is still an energy-intensive process that requires extensive transportation and waste processing. It is better to take advantage of materials as they are, without adding to the carbon burden that has already been generated by their manufacture.

The greenest object is one that already exists. If something is built to last, it doesn't need to be thrown into a landfill. Physical durability is the easy part; it's more difficult to design for aesthetic durability, so that an object can age gracefully. Since wear is inevitable, tastes change, and the future is hard to predict, the best guerilla designs are repairable, hackable, and robust. Nearly every project in this book breaks down into constituent parts, ready for recycling, reuse, or wholesale reinvention.

In the world of manufacturing, planned obsolescence ensures consumers will keep spending money on new products. However, the guerilla can creatively bend obsolescence to sustainable ends. Used for a short period of time (say, two college semesters), a cardboard chair can be recycled instead of lugged home and stored for another year (saving the carbon footprint of all that transportation!). When glued with all-natural wheat paste, cardboard can be recycled, composted, or burned — no landfill needed. For longer-lived projects, the life cycle must still be taken into account. Dissimilar materials, like wood and metal, are joined with bolts so components can be separated and reused or discarded appropriately. If the piece is still functional, taking it to a thrift store is always a good option.

There's an old story, perhaps apocryphal, about the U.S. and Soviet space programs during the Cold War. The Americans, looking for a way for astronauts to write in the cold, zero-gravity Mercury capsules, spent millions of dollars developing a pressurized space pen. The Russians used a pencil. The guerilla takes a pencil approach to sustainability: frugality, durability, and (responsible) disposability.

GUERILLA PHILOSOPHY

My education as a designer and craftsman has followed two parallel tracks: the academic study of design and the practical study of building arts. Formal design disciplines, created several centuries ago, developed a fault line between those who design and those who *make*. Our culture tends to regard the former as somehow intellectually superior, ignoring the mental complexity inherent in manual work.

Consumerist culture has further reinforced these fault lines, as individuals find themselves radically separated from the processes that sustain them. We have little understanding of where our food comes from, how water finds its way to our faucets, or who made the shiny screens in our pockets. The infrastructure of the world has become confounding, full of misfiring automatic doors, nonflushing touchless toilets, baffling thermostats. We increasingly interact with virtual interfaces and faceless people, disconnected from the physical realm.

As our culture sinks into incomprehensibility, design and construction become a means by which we can understand the world around us. Reclaiming manual competency satisfies the fundamental human urge to make sense of our environment, grounded in the grit of splinters, sawdust, and muttered curses. Hand-building furniture (or anything else) is also a political act — a practical protest against corporate hegemony, environmental destruction, and individual apathy. Building as an act of resistance flips the usual paradigm of protest, creating positive products instead of merely tearing down the status quo.

However, the practice of disciplined craft is not a violent pursuit. *Guerilla*, as used in this book, refers not to a warrior so much as an *irregular*, or one who stands in opposition to societal customs. As an irregular, I choose to exempt myself from certain aspects of consumer culture in favor of *doing it myself*. In my work, I attempt to adhere to the following four values.

ONE
ECONOMY

Each project in this book is an exercise in material, visual, and fiscal efficiency, built from the by-products of the modern consumer-industrial complex. A guerilla designer should maximize resources, minimize waste, and leverage available assets.

TWO
HONESTY

Materials bear a patina of time and marks made by the passage of human hands, thus communicating their history and potential. A guerilla designer should obtain material honestly and treat it respectfully, avoiding elaborate ornamentation or obscuring finishes.

THREE
UTILITY

Furniture is a functional art meant to solve a number of mundane, practical problems. A guerilla designer should strive for ergonomic, stable, structurally sound solutions.

FOUR
BEAUTY

Beauty is, of course, subjective and elusive. However, if a design is spare, honest, and useful, it often ends up being beautiful by nature. The guerilla designer should develop coherence of form, color, craftsmanship, and conceptual idea.

"PROCEED AND BE BOLD."

SAMUEL MOCKBEE

THE GUERILLA WORKSHOP

I have moved once a year for the last six years. Not everyone bounces around quite so much, but technology and a shifty economy certainly have made folks more mobile than in the past, while the housing collapse has created a new class of renters. However, moving frequently and renting need not crimp your ability to build furniture — workshops can be improvised anywhere with an extension cord and a little creativity.

The places I've lived in over the years have varied widely: a wide-open loft, a few rooms rented out of a larger house, a two-bedroom above a copy shop, a tight Chicago studio, and a big, communal apartment at Arcosanti. All of them lacked storage space or much room to make a mess, but each had an accessory space where I found a way to do my work. Here are some ideas for carving out a workspace in tight quarters.

Storage unit When living in an urban apartment building, there is usually a basement storage space allotted to each unit. This can be a perfect place to put some tools, materials, or finished pieces. If the storage space has walls, it can contain the dust and noise of a few circular saw cuts. Cut and prepare material in the basement, then bring it upstairs to the apartment for clean assembly.

Porch or deck While attending school in Alabama, I lived in four rooms carved out of an antebellum house. I had an impromptu workspace on the screened side porch, setting up sawhorses to sand a tabletop. Porches and decks are great — protected from rain, well ventilated, and within private property lines. Lay down flattened cardboard boxes to protect the floor, and run an extension cord through the screen door. In good weather, a flat patio can serve the same function.

Garage This is a natural home workshop. The Internet and home-improvement magazines are full of plans for turning a two-car garage into a pro-grade woodshop. However, the guerilla doesn't have to own a home to have access to that kind of space. Cities, especially those with alley networks, are full of garages, many for rent. Apartments in subdivided houses often have common garages. Set up a temporary space with two sawhorses, a sheet of plywood, and a power strip, breaking down and sweeping up when the project is finished.

Extra room Spare rooms or living rooms are the last resort for the guerilla. Cutting wood in a living space is deafening, dirty, and mildly dangerous. That said, lots of projects can be completed safely indoors, in the comforting presence of a TV and full refrigerator. Most of the cardboard projects in this book are easy to do indoors; just use a cutting mat to prevent scarring the floor. If a messy process must be attempted, try to clear out upholstered furniture, shut doors, and lay down some plastic to protect the space. Sawdust, or smoke created by an overheated blade or bit, can set off smoke alarms, so set up a fan pointing out through an open window to vent any dust and smoke. A little prevention goes a long way toward retaining a security deposit.

Makerspaces

In recent years, makerspaces have begun to pop up in many cities. They offer access to industrial-grade woodworking, metalworking, and electronics equipment in exchange for a membership fee. Many require members to take a basic competency class before turning them loose on the tools. The cost may be an up-front barrier, but makerspaces offer great gear, tech support, and the space to get messy, as well as an opportunity to meet other DIYers in your area. For simpler projects, take your cut list to the hardware store and they will slice up the material for you for a small fee, though the accuracy may be less than superb.

Outdoors Weather permitting, the great outdoors can be the best workshop of all. With a little level ground, some sunshine, and a solid extension cord, working outside is great. Cleanup is minimal and ventilation is superb. Working on various job-sites over the years, I've set up chop saws in alleys, clients' backyards, and even on flat roofs. Just be mindful of generating sparks, blocking traffic, or falling off the parapet.

TOOLS

The guerilla fighter has traditionally armed himself with the simplest of weapons, improvised from common materials or scavenged from the field of battle. The guerilla maker does the same. Don't believe the pushy, aproned folks at the hardware store; you need only a very basic tool kit to build the furniture in this book (specialized tools are discussed further in each Tools section). When you do buy, invest in good tools that will last a long time. Quality equipment is available on Craigslist, eBay, or through manufacturer-certified resellers at decent prices.

Hand tools Start with the basics: a sharp pencil, a tape measure, a square, and a box cutter. Get a metal-bodied tape, at least 20 feet long, and a metal Speed Square, a right triangle marked with angle measurements along the hypotenuse. A combination square, consisting of a ruler and a sliding square piece with built-in level, is also very helpful. A solid metal-bodied box cutter with breakaway blades is indispensable for every kind of project. Protective glasses, tight-fitting work gloves (so loose fabric doesn't get caught in moving parts), and earmuffs round out the safety gear.

Other hand tools crop up frequently: adjustable wrench, ratchet set, needle-nose pliers, end pliers (for de-nailing scrap lumber), small crowbar, flat-head screwdriver, block plane, chisels, hammer, and clamps.

Good hand tools last generations, and can be found at flea markets and secondhand shops. Old tools are often preferable, solidly made of hardwood and heavy steel. Polish off surface rust with light oil and steel wool. Wooden handles can be revived with 220-grit sandpaper and tung oil.

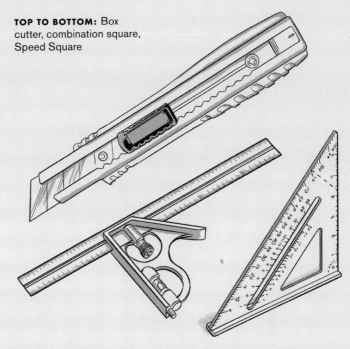

TOP TO BOTTOM: Box cutter, combination square, Speed Square

Power tools Power tools are expensive and bulky. If lacking storage and/or cash, borrow! Many a homeowner has an old saw in the basement they'd be happy to part with for a few hours. Ask neighbors, friends, and family. A quick search online may also find a tool library in your area, which may lend out tools temporarily in exchange for a small membership fee. Big-box hardware stores also offer short-term tool rentals, perfect for discrete tasks like sanding a tabletop.

Tool storage I keep my tools in two break-pack totes — plastic chests used to transport small merchandise to stores. You can buy these cheaply at big-box hardware stores. I added plywood dividers to keep things organized, and the containers lock together for easy stacking. Another tote holds fasteners, wire, tape, washers, nails, and glue, all sorted in plastic tubs. A toolbox should be arranged so that everything is accessible without moving anything else (what Adam Savage, of MythBusters, calls *first-order accessibility*). Lacking break-packs, use an old footlocker or milk crates, or build a plywood box. Keep fasteners in peanut butter jars, coffee cans, mint tins, or plastic tubs. If you know you are going to be moving often, invest in a used hand truck, stack on the totes, and roll the shop away.

THE CITY IS A FERTILE ENVIRONMENT FOR THE DESIGN GUERILLA, OFFERING VISUAL INSPIRATION, CULTURAL RESOURCES, AND ABUNDANT FORAGING GROUNDS.

Design tools The guerilla, however, is not only a builder; he is also a designer, documentarian, and micro-architect. I design mostly by hand, drawing on napkins and bits of lumber, then proper paper. Use whatever sketchbook you find most comfortable and a black felt-tip pen to record and refine ideas. I keep a small, pocket-size notebook and a letter-size, graph-paper drawing pad by Rhodia, which enables scale drawings.

To figure out tough questions of ergonomics or aesthetics, it can be helpful to make full-size drawings. Use chalk, a square, and a straightedge to draft designs on the garage floor. Creating small-scale models is another way to figure out tricky processes, like bending road signs. Use cereal-box chipboard to prototype different folding schemes before applying the design to the metal.

A wide variety of drawing apps are now available for tablets and phones, as well as free 3-D modeling software like SketchUp. Smartphones enable the guerilla to document the work. I photograph my drawings, for reference, and then snap pictures of every step of the build process. These photos (and sometimes videos) are invaluable in the future, allowing you to both remember and further refine the process. One-touch uploads to Tumblr, Facebook, Twitter, or other online outlets allow you to save and share your work, expanding the community of makers.

MATERIAL FORAGING

The city is a fertile environment for the design guerilla, offering visual inspiration, cultural resources, and abundant foraging grounds. Density of population produces a density of *stuff*, and that stuff tends to collect at certain pinch points. To save money and landfill space, the guerilla can mine these seams in the urban fabric for raw material.

Successful foraging begins at home. Many projects in this book rely on patient accumulation of junk — plastic bags, pill bottles, cardboard boxes. Once a critical mass is achieved, the pile can be processed into a new form. However, don't let saving veer into hoarding. Guerillas are lightweight nomads and harvest only what they need for the project at hand.

Bigger materials, like plywood or two-by-fours, have to be sought out in the world. Many big cities have extensive alley networks, which are a gold mine of potential material. Homeowners embarking on maintenance projects or cleaning out their garages leave scrap lumber in the alley. After Christmas, and during summer moving season, stacks of flattened corrugated boxes appear tucked behind trashcans. Old furniture can be broken down and used as lumber — think shelves, tabletops, or chair legs. Treat your alleys and neighbors well, staying on the roadway and leaving things neater than you found them. Bring a utility knife and work gloves to break down boxes in the field.

New residential construction usually involves a roll-off dumpster. In urban areas, where small lots are crowded, the dumpsters are parked on the street. Anything in a dumpster on the public way is fair game, and it is often full of usable lengths of lumber. Demolition of older buildings provides better scrap, at longer lengths, than new construction, where the trash heap is mostly short offcuts. Don't hesitate to ask a carpenter on-site to look through their scrap pile — they pay to get rid of it and are usually happy to see someone take it away for free.

College campuses are the best of both worlds: they are in a constant state of both construction and population turnover. At the end of each semester, check dorm dumpsters for the latest in futons, storage systems, and lamps. Lights are great — strip switches, sockets, and wire out of the cheap fixture housing. Futon frames provide long, straight runs of prefinished lumber that is easy to repurpose. Campuses are largely abandoned on the weekends, as staff and faculty stay home, providing an opportune time to explore construction dumpsters. Engineering and art department dumpsters tend to accumulate more lumber, metal, and interesting bits of cardboard. Use the campus map signboards to locate the most promising hunting grounds.

In the suburbs, resources may be more spread out. In communities that lack alleys, prowl cul-de-sacs for yard sales. The county dump or transfer station may allow scavenging from open dumpsters (check with the manager). In rural Alabama, I stumbled into a great trove of old road signs by merely asking (very politely!) at the county engineer's office. Strip malls generate vast amounts of paper waste. Drive around the back of the buildings, and each store usually has a cardboard dumpster or a baling machine. Look especially at furniture and electronics retailers, where big, heavy, double-wall corrugated boxes are the norm. Just a few fridge-sized boxes are big enough to build a chair. Pallets collect around loading docks. Since they have to bear a lot of weight, pallets are usually made from hardwood, like oak or poplar. Though difficult to de-nail, pallets are a great source of free lumber.

Most malls will have cameras and a security car, but I have never been bothered; I guess nobody wants to mess with a dumpster diver. Should you be stopped by a security officer, tell them you are collecting refuse left on the public way. If they insist, just leave. There are other alleys to roam.

Of course, the modern guerilla doesn't just stalk alleys hoping to get lucky. Craigslist, Freecycle, and eBay are other great resources. Bookmark the "free" section of Craigslist and check it regularly. Freecycle, while not in as many cities, is guaranteed to only have free stuff. When looking for something specific — say, a wheelbarrow shell — post a wanted ad on Craigslist, offering to haul it away. For projects that require a lot of little, repeated items that take time to collect, ask around on Facebook or Twitter. If friends are collecting on your behalf, you can amass 50 pill bottles (see Pill Bottle Pendant Lamp on page 135) in a fraction of the time it might take to stockpile them yourself.

The venerable ol' Goodwill or Salvation Army stores have solid hunks of furniture that cost very little. Disassembled, they are a cheap source of hardwood. Salvage warehouses, which offer the guts of deconstructed buildings, have been springing up all over the place. Habitat for Humanity has opened a national salvage warehouse chain, called ReStore, whose profits are recycled into more Habitat houses.

As the guerilla becomes more experienced, materials seem to appear everywhere. A daily dog walk becomes a foraging trip, slipping into alleys and under train tracks. A grocery run will include a quick detour behind the building, packing the backseat with cardboard boxes. The drive to work will turn into reconnaissance, scanning the curbs for old furniture. The practiced forager never stops looking, eyes open for fresh opportunities.

DESIGN FUNDAMENTALS

Furniture design is a complex triangulation, balancing ergonomics, structure, and form. Guerilla furniture design builds upon these fundamental principles, layering in the use of salvaged materials and unconventional building techniques in the pursuit of inexpensive, sustainable solutions. As you move beyond the case studies in this book and begin designing your own pieces, keep in mind that the process is as important as the product. Iterate repeatedly on paper, then prototype repeatedly in built form, and solid designs will eventually emerge from the sawdust and pencil shavings.

THE HUMAN FORM

Humans come in an astonishing variety of shapes, sizes, and colors, yet there is an equally astonishing similarity in the measure of bodies and limbs across the human spectrum. Accordingly, building codes and manufacturing standards have codified a set of dimensions that rule our world. American architects and other design professionals routinely turn to two resources — *Architectural Graphic Standards* and the *International Building Code* — for everything from the width of doorways to the height of countertops.

Much of the information in *AGS* and the *IBC* is based on a single work, *The Measure of Man*, first published in 1959 by industrial designer Henry Dreyfuss. The raw data used to write that book was drawn from records collected by the U.S. Army during World War II as the government processed millions of recruits. Because the soldiers were all men in a certain age range, the data were skewed, ignoring women, children, the elderly, and the disabled. Over time, and many revisions, that sample has been broadened. The dimensions laid out in *AGS* and building codes throughout the country are meant to accommodate the most people as comfortably as possible.

The projects in this book use a combination of established standards and rules learned through years of experimentation. Mass-manufactured products have not arrived at their dimensions by accident; they have been carefully tested and examined. In that sense, the world is filled with research subjects. When in doubt, merely take a tape measure to yourself or the furniture around you to confirm proportions.

STRUCTURE AND STABILITY

Force arrives in three forms: *compression*, *tension*, and *shear*. Compression, familiar to all of us as gravity, is the direct downward application of pressure. This causes a structural member to deform by crushing or bending until it breaks. Tension, familiar to all of us as stretching, is the direct application of *pulling* pressure. This causes a structural member to elongate until it gives way. Compression and tension work in perpendicular alignments. Shear is any force that is not perpendicular or parallel to a surface or structural member. It is what causes a square bookcase to lean into a parallelogram over time. All furniture, through material and form, needs to resist these three forces.

"A CHAIR IS A LITTLE PIECE OF ARCHITECTURE THAT ONE MAN CAN HANDLE."
CHARLES EAMES

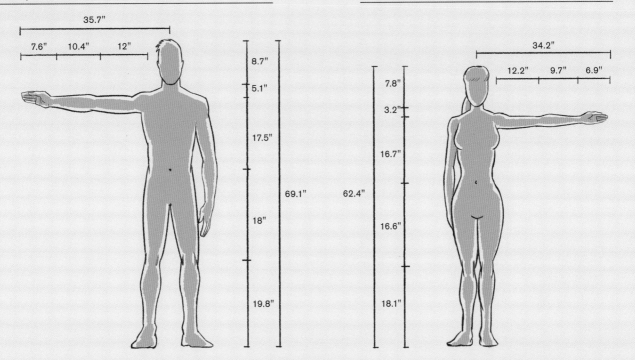

MAN, 162 LBS.

35.7"

7.6" 10.4" 12"

8.7"
5.1"
17.5"
18"
19.8"

69.1"

WOMAN, 133.5 LBS.

34.2"

12.2" 9.7" 6.9"

7.8"
3.2"
16.7"
16.6"
18.1"

62.4"

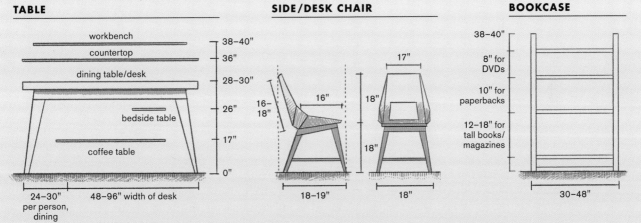

TABLE

workbench — 38–40"
countertop — 36"
dining table/desk — 28–30"
— 26"
bedside table
— 17"
coffee table
— 0"

24–30"
per person,
dining

48–96" width of desk

SIDE/DESK CHAIR

17"

16–18" 16" 18"

18"

18–19" 18"

BOOKCASE

38–40"

8" for
DVDs

10" for
paperbacks

12–18" for
tall books/
magazines

30–48"

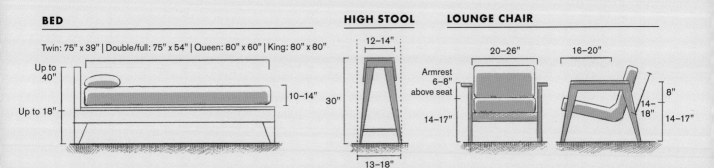

BED

Twin: 75" x 39" | Double/full: 75" x 54" | Queen: 80" x 60" | King: 80" x 80"

Up to 40"

Up to 18"

10–14"

HIGH STOOL

12–14"

30"

13–18"

LOUNGE CHAIR

20–26" 16–20"

Armrest
6–8"
above seat

14–17"

8"

14–18"

14–17"

16

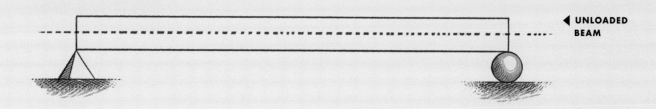

◀ **UNLOADED BEAM**

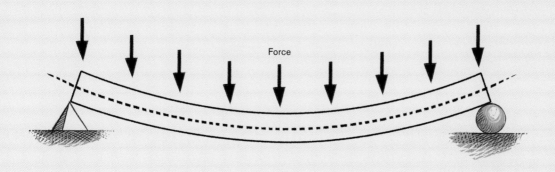

Force

◀ **COMPRESSION** A direct downward application of force compresses the top side of the beam and stretches the underside until the failure point is reached.

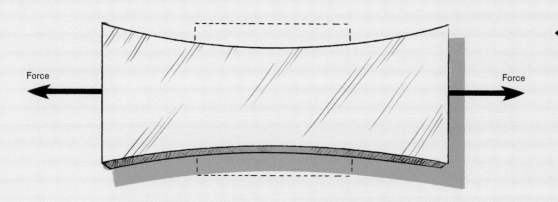

Force

Force

◀ **TENSION** Pulling forces stretch the material to the failure point.

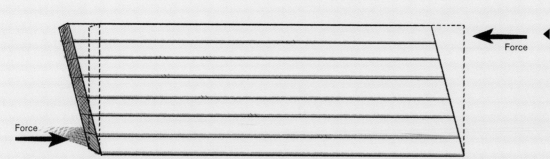

Force

Force

◀ **SHEAR** Asymmetric forces deform the material from opposing directions.

Forces are applied to structures by two types of loads. A *live load* is the force generated by the occupant of the furniture — a person in a chair or books on a shelf. A *dead load* is the mass of the structure itself. A simple understanding of these forces illustrates why furniture is built the way it is.

Tables are straightforward structures, consisting of a flat, elevated surface. They generally receive little compressive force — the weight of the tabletop itself is usually the greatest load. However, they do need to be able to support the weight of someone occasionally sitting or standing on top of them.

Tables usually have four legs, relatively tall, spread quite far apart. Each leg wants to go its own way, shearing left or right. To lock them in place, most tables rely on an *apron*, a set of boards that run around the perimeter of the underside of the table, locking the legs to the tabletop and to one another. Triangulating a brace off each leg, in each direction, will prevent the leg from moving.

Tenoning (see page 18) buries the leg in the tabletop to lock it in place. A *tenon* is a carved projection that fits into a corresponding *mortise*, or hole. The *shoulders* of the tenon then bear against the underside of the tabletop, counteracting wobble. A tension member at the base of the legs prevents them from spreading outward under load. A *trestle* table consists of two transverse supports linked by a longitudinal member, a strategy most commonly seen in basic wooden picnic tables.

Chairs are the most complex pieces of furniture. They have to deal with asymmetrically applied, ever-shifting, widely varying loads. People sit on people's laps. People stand on chairs to change light bulbs. People tip back chairs on their rear legs. These people also come in a wide variety of shapes and sizes, weighing hundreds of pounds.

The simplest concern with chairs is compression. Disregarding the back for a moment, a chair is essentially a small table, with a lot of weight

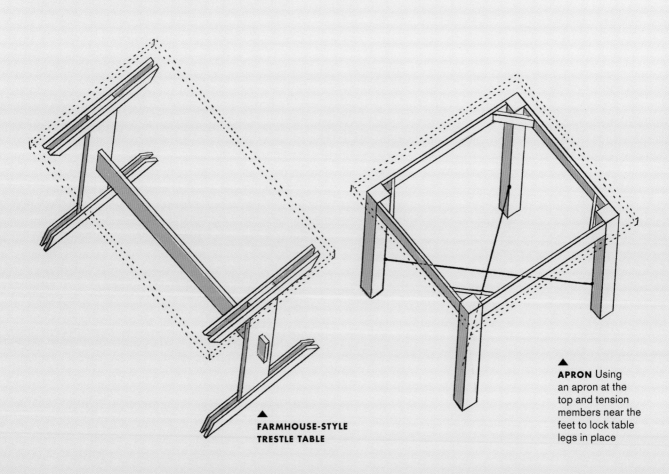

▲
FARMHOUSE-STYLE TRESTLE TABLE

▲
APRON Using an apron at the top and tension members near the feet to lock table legs in place

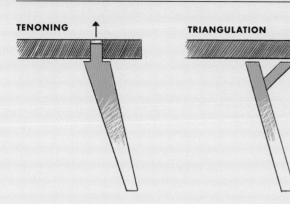

TENONING

TRIANGULATION

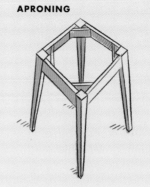

APRONING

BOX FRAME

CONSTRUCTION TECHNIQUES FOR CHAIRS

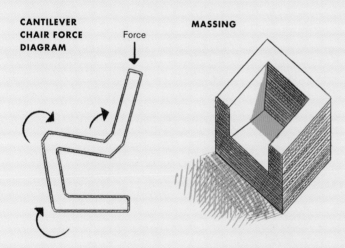

CANTILEVER CHAIR FORCE DIAGRAM

Force

MASSING

concentrated on a small surface area. The legs have to be strong enough to take 200-plus pounds. With wood, this means orienting force along the long grain, or using plywood joined at right angles to create a stiff cross-section. In cardboard chairs, legs are replaced with a stable mass of laminated or folded material (called *massing*). Techniques for preventing the legs from wobbling are the same as in tables — tenoning, aproning, triangulating, and tying the legs together at the bottom.

Chair backs must resist a compound array of forces, combining shear and tension. For ergonomic reasons, the back is tilted at a slight angle, predisposing it to failure. The best way to counteract these problems is to make the back support a continuous part of the seat, forming an "L" when viewed from the side. That way the back cannot tilt rearward without lifting the seat, which is counterbalanced by the weight of the sitter. This "L" unit can then be mounted to legs in any manner of ways.

The most complex type of chair is a cantilever, which eliminates back legs altogether. Without four legs bearing weight to the ground, the whole structure works in tension. When loaded, the back pulls against the seat, which pulls against the front legs, which pulls up on the floor assembly. This extraordinary stress requires careful construction and material selection.

Shelves Even in the age of cloud content, folks own books, records, DVDs, and other shelve-able media. Books, in aggregate, are extremely heavy, to the point where libraries need reinforced foundation systems. Shelves need to bear significant compressive forces while resisting the shear that might make them lean sideways over time.

Shelves love to sag — even heavy planks bow toward the center over time. To stiffen them, build each shelf like a framing system of joists and floor decking. Turn one board on edge (joist), and fasten it to a flat board (floor), creating a T-shaped cross section. The board set on edge will resist deflection and the flat board provides a level surface. Building an open-topped box and flipping it over achieves the same end.

Shear will gradually push a square bookcase into a parallelogram over time. This is most commonly counteracted with a continuous (*diaphragm*) back — a sheet of plywood or hardboard attached to all four corners of the bookcase. An *X-brace*, using tension elements to span corner-to-corner, also works, but may make it more difficult to get the assembly square. Shelves themselves can act as bracing when bolted securely to the upright members of the structure, forming a solid connection (or *moment connection*, in engineer-speak) that resists racking from side to side.

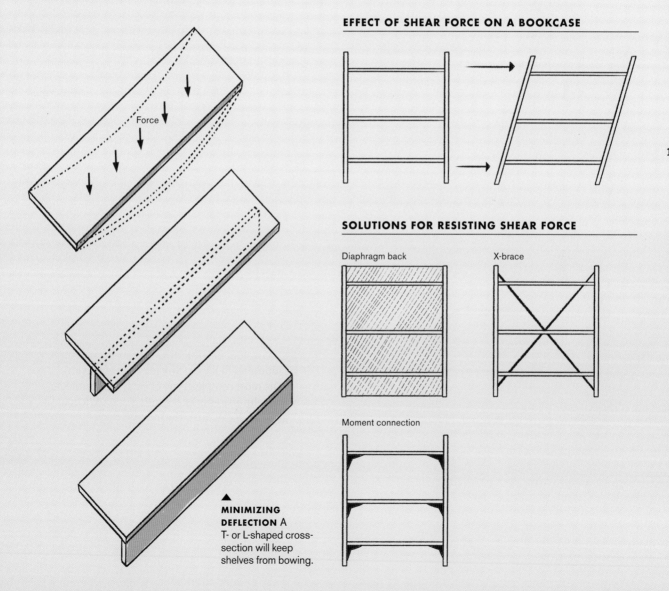

Force

EFFECT OF SHEAR FORCE ON A BOOKCASE

SOLUTIONS FOR RESISTING SHEAR FORCE

Diaphragm back

X-brace

Moment connection

▲ **MINIMIZING DEFLECTION** A T- or L-shaped cross-section will keep shelves from bowing.

PAPER IS THE IDEAL MATERIAL FOR THE GUERILLA DESIGNER.

It's light, plentiful, and recyclable. It passes through our daily lives in many forms, from paper bags to the rapidly disappearing newspaper. The average American flushes about 26 rolls of toilet paper every year.

For thousands of years, people wrote on clay tablets, reed mats, and animal skins. Pulp-based paper was first developed in the second century by court scholars of the Han dynasty in China, spreading from there through Islamic kingdoms of the Middle East and on to the West. Until the nineteenth century, paper remained an expensive commodity because it was made by hand out of scarce cloth rags. In 1844, Charles Fenerty, of Canada, and F. G. Keller, a German, both invented processes for pulping wood fiber for paper manufacture. Over time, water-powered pulping mills, supplied by America's vast forests, dropped the price of paper to a point where it became a disposable commodity.

Paper production begins with *pulping* wood, either chemically or mechanically, rendering solid wood chips into long, stringy bundles of cellulose fiber. *Chemical pulping* removes the *lignin*, a compound found in the cell walls of plants that weakens paper and causes it to yellow over time. The *kraft process* uses a mixture of water, sodium sulfide, and sodium hydroxide to remove the lignin, rendering a pure mash of cellulose fibers. Chemical pulping, while less efficient, produces a better-quality fiber used in printing, archival, and book papers. *Mechanical pulping* just grinds up the wood and washes it with water. It is a cheaper, higher-yield process but produces a brittle product suitable for boxes and newsprint.

Paper can be used by the guerilla in a variety of ways. Saturated with paste, paper becomes papier-mâché, allowing the construction of hard, durable shells in fluid shapes. Corrugated cardboard can be laminated and then worked like wood, creating a sturdy lumber substitute. Alternatively, intersecting grids of corrugated cardboard are strong enough to support substantial amounts of weight. The heavy cardboard tubes at the center of rolls

of plotter paper, newsprint, or fabric are incredibly strong, can hold bolts and screws, and finish well with wax or polyurethane. Bigger cardboard tubes, like the ones used for concrete formwork (Sonotube is one common product), can be made into seating and storage with little modification.

Paper is also the perfect introductory material for the beginner craftsman. It is cheap (often free), easy to work, requires limited tools, and provides the aspiring designer with the means to rapidly prototype ideas. We will examine many permanent furniture projects made of paper here, but cardboard also makes a great material for models, patterns, and templates.

MATERIALS

NEWSPRINT

Newsprint is a low-quality, low-strength gray paper made by mechanically pulping wood. A low sulfur content makes it susceptible to yellowing, and it will become brittle and flaky over time, especially when exposed to sunlight. As the name would suggest, it is most widely used for printing newspapers and other disposable paper products. It can also be bought, unprinted, on rolls. Artists use it for sketching, and designers use it to template for dresses and other fabric goods. Its cheapness, absorbency, and wide availability (often for free) make it a great material for papier-mâché, though it takes many layers to build up strength. It readily absorbs paint and other finishes.

KRAFT PAPER

Kraft paper is a dense, coarse brown paper used in envelopes, grocery bags, corrugated cardboard, shotgun cartridges, and as backing for sandpaper. It has a high tensile (tearing) strength, which makes it good for bags, boxes, and other packaging. A high sulfur content makes it resistant to yellowing. It can be bought on 24" or 36" rolls at hardware stores, office-supply stores, and shipping companies. The

most widely available free source is grocery bags; cut along the seams and unfolded, bags provide 2 to 3 square feet of material. Kraft paper works well for high-strength papier-mâché, though its slightly hydrophilic nature makes it harder to saturate with glue. Once dried hard, it can be sanded and shaped like softwood.

ROSIN PAPER

Rosin paper is a heavyweight kraft paper impregnated with rosin, the resin of softwood trees. This imbues it with a reddish tint and a degree of water resistance. Builders use it as underlayment for wooden floors or a temporary protective surface over floors and windows during construction. It is very strong and resistant to tearing but doesn't glue well due to its water resistance.

PAPERBOARD

Paperboard encompasses a dozen or so subcategories, though it generally refers to thin, kraft-based cardboard in common items like cereal boxes. Chipboard specifically refers to recycled paperboard. It comes in different thicknesses made of laminated layers known as plies. A single ply is about $\frac{1}{16}$" thick, and may be laminated up to eight times to create pieces as thick as $\frac{1}{4}$".

Chipboard can be found at craft and art supply stores, commonly sold in 30" × 40" sheets. It is used in architectural model making, packaging, and fine-art poster printing.

CORRUGATED CARDBOARD

Corrugated cardboard was first mass-manufactured in the 1870s, initially as single-face sheets used to protect delicate objects during shipping. About 20 years later, the first double-faced sheets were used to make pre-creased foldable boxes, still in wide use today. The fluted middle layer of double-faced cardboard provides much of the material's strength. When force is applied in line with the "grain," parallel to the flutes, corrugated cardboard can bear considerable weight.

Single-wall cardboard has two face sheets and one layer of corrugation. Double-wall cardboard has two face sheets and two layers or corrugation, with a third flat sheet in between, creating a stronger, more rigid material than single-wall cardboard. In recent years, packaging companies have designed advanced corrugation patterns, such as honeycomb boards, for specialty applications.

Corrugated can be bought in flat sheets from craft stores and shipping companies, but the best source of corrugated is flattened boxes, abundant in alleys and behind big-box stores.

HARDBOARD

Hardboard (often referred to by the brand name Masonite) is not technically a paper product, but it is made with a similar process and works well in concert with cardboard. Invented in 1924 by William Mason, it is made by pressure-cooking wood fibers with steam and then bonding them under pressure, resulting in a thin uniform sheet. The lignin in the fiber serves as an adhesive, eliminating glue from the lamination process. It is used for crating artwork, as a painting surface, skins for skateboard ramps, mold-making, and other applications where a flexible, smooth surface is desired. Hardboard comes in ⅛" and ¼" thicknesses, with one smooth side and one rough side. Thin, inexpensive, nontoxic, and uniform, it glues well and makes an excellent diaphragm back for shelves or cabinets. The lack of glue means it is generally safe to use with laser cutters, though it smells awful when burned.

HOMASOTE

Homasote is a brand name for compressed cellulose board. Generally ½" thick, it consists of shredded recycled paper fiber compressed with heat and adhesive to form flat sheets. The result is a strong, porous board that is essentially a giant sheet of papier-mâché. It has excellent sound-deadening and thermal insulation qualities and is often used as a pin board. It is soft and easy to work but produces a fine, clingy dust when cut. Use a regular circular saw with a finishing blade for cuts, and fasten with slip-fit drywall screws and wood glue.

PAPER TUBES

Paper tubes are found at the center of rolls of material, from toilet paper to newsprint. Thicker-walled cardboard tubes found at the center of big rolls of paper are an ideal structural material — extremely strong, light, and already formed into a linear structural unit. Cardboard tubes are much like lumber in that they can hold mechanical fasteners like screws and react well to wood finishes like polyurethane. Look for tubes at print shops, shipping companies, or architecture firms that print large-format drawings. Long fluorescent lights come packaged in thick-walled paper tubes; look for tubes in dumpsters around office complexes and construction sites. Mailing tubes typically are too lightweight for structural uses but, like corrugated cardboard, may be strong enough to bear weight when massed.

WHEAT PASTE

Wheat paste is a glue that takes advantage of the adhesive properties of gluten, a protein found in wheat and other grains. It can be made for cents on the gallon and kept in the refrigerator until needed. Historically, it has been used as wallpaper paste and poster adhesive. It can be used to both stick material together and saturate it to provide a degree of water-resistance and durability. Diluted wheat paste is used to create papier-mâché.

Making Your Own Wheat Paste

Add five parts water to a saucepan and set it on high to boil. While the water is heating, dissolve one part flour into one part cold water by gradually adding the flour and whisking constantly.

When the water boils, add the flour-water mixture to the pan, again whisking constantly. Return to a boil for 30 to 60 seconds. It should thicken somewhat, but don't be alarmed if it appears thin; it will thicken further as it cools. Remove the pan from the heat and let the paste cool to room temperature before use.

Adding a few tablespoons of sugar at the end of the boiling (so the sugar doesn't burn) increases stickiness, which is helpful because plain wheat paste doesn't have much "grab" when wet. The same amount of salt or vinegar acts as a preservative to increase shelf life. For a stronger, thicker paste, increase the proportion of flour or use whole-wheat flour, which contains more gluten than white flour. If you can't use all of the paste immediately, you can refrigerate it for up to a week; let it come up to room temperature and whisk out any chunks or coagulated "skin" before using.

TOOLS

PAINTBRUSH

A paintbrush is the go-to tool for spreading wheat paste. Buy a decent-quality synthetic-bristle brush, and wash it out thoroughly with hot water between uses. Foam brushes are a little too flimsy to stand up to the thick glue.

STRAIGHTEDGE

Cutting straight lines in cardboard freehand is nearly impossible. Invest in a metal yardstick or drywall T-square, or use a metal spirit level as a straightedge to make clean cuts.

BOX CUTTER

The most indispensable tool for working with cardboard is a good box cutter. Available at any hardware store, the best box cutters have a metal body and use breakaway blades, allowing you to snap off segments as they become dull. You can also extend the blade to cut through multiple layers of material. Use a cutter in tandem with a good-quality straightedge for true cuts. Take it with you when stalking alleys for material so you can break down boxes in the field.

CLAMPS

Laminating cardboard can be challenging, as the material is not rigid enough to distribute clamping pressure, leaving air pockets and weak spots. When gluing strips together, sandwich them between 2×4s or other scrap lumber to compress the cardboard evenly. Clamps are not cheap, but it is worth investing in four or five 24" bar clamps that can be used for multiple projects.

SAWS

When laminated, corrugated cardboard acts much like lumber — it can be cut, drilled, and sanded. A circular saw, table saw, or jigsaw allows for straight, precise cuts through many layers of glue-saturated (thoroughly dried) material with a lot less labor than a box cutter. Some sort of power saw is also essential for cutting harder paper products, such as hardboard or Homasote. Use a fine-toothed finishing blade for smooth cuts and minimal tear-out. See Wood (chapter) for more information on using power saws with wood.

METHODS

LAMINATION

Lamination refers to the gluing of many layers of material together to make a thicker sheet. Cardboard and paper are particularly well suited to lamination, which helps to capitalize on their strengths and minimize their weaknesses. Large sheets of cardboard "plywood" can be manufactured by gluing corrugated cardboard together with wheat paste, alternating the direction of the corrugations with each layer. Spread the glue with a brush or roller on both faces (except the top- and bottom-most layers) of each cardboard sheet and press the pieces together on a flat surface. Stack a piece of plywood on top and weight evenly with bricks, cinderblocks, sandbags, etc. Let it dry for 24 hours, preferably with a fan circulating air. Wheat paste (see page 25 for recipe) is made of organic ingredients and can take a long time to dry, which may lead to moldy cardboard if left damp for too long. Once the glue has dried hard, the resultant material can be worked like wood.

Protect your working surface with scrap cardboard or a drop cloth, as wheat paste tends to get everywhere. Work as quickly as possible to ensure the pile is under clamping pressure before the glue on the first layer begins to dry, which can result in delamination. If a very thick sheet is desired, make a series of smaller laminations (say, five sheets each), let dry, then glue up a stack of five-ply pieces.

Stack lamination refers to the practice of precutting layers of material to size and shape *before* gluing them together. This process can save time and minimize waste when gluing up curved or unusual shapes. The trick is getting everything aligned as the glue dries. Use a template to cut all your pieces, including a pattern of registration holes – holes that are in the same location in every layer – and slide the pieces onto dowels. Once all the pieces are in place, withdraw the dowels and weight the stack. Alternately, build a plywood formwork that holds the edges of all the pieces in alignment as the pile progresses.

Dry lamination is glueless laminating, using mechanical fasteners, ratchet straps, twine, or tape to bind together disparate layers of cardboard into a structurally cohesive unit. A simple example is the bales of waste cardboard behind every supermarket; boxes are flattened, compressed, and bundled with nylon or metal strips. Homemade bales, bound with twisted twine, can be made into seed-starter bricks or basic benches. Flat sheets can be rolled up into coils and taped (neatly) into very strong structural columns.

Curved stack lamination for design objects was pioneered in the 1940s by Charles and Ray Eames. Thin veneers of wood were pressed into curved forms with adhesive, and then cured under heat and pressure, resulting in organic shapes. The same process can be employed on a guerilla scale by clamping cardboard into shaped formwork with copious amounts of wheat paste. Curved lamination is a form of pre-stressing, which has ergonomic and structural advantages. Arching the material makes it more resistant to compression without increasing mass.

FOLDED STRUCTURES

Origami is an ancient Japanese art in which thin sheets of paper are folded into animals, flowers, and complex geometric abstractions. Cardboard, with the help of slits and creases, can be made into structural, load-bearing shapes without the use of tape or glue. Score corrugated cardboard lightly, along the grain, to facilitate folding. Secure the folds with a system of tabs and slots, pin in place with coarse-thread drywall screws, or "sew" together with zip ties. Orient the flutes in line with the application of force for maximum load-bearing capacity. For instance, in a stool or chair, the flutes should run vertically to resist the weight of the sitter.

PAPIER-MÂCHÉ

Papier-mâché has a long history – linen dipped in plaster was used to make death masks of the pharaohs in ancient Egypt. In the eighteenth and nineteenth centuries, papier-mâché panels treated with lacquer or linseed oil were used to make lightweight body panels for carriages. Modern papier-mâché typically is made with strips of newsprint saturated with wheat paste and laid over a form, where it dries into a hard, durable shell. Strengthen the basic wheat paste mix (page 25) by adding small amounts of plaster or PVA (white) glue. Shape the finished pieces with sandpaper and finish with rubbed oil, polyurethane, or paint.

PAPER TUBE JOINERY

Paper tubes have a high strength-to-weight ratio, but their round cross-section makes them difficult to join together. They can be saddled together with notches, similar to log cabin construction, and secured with a machine bolt pin. Spline joinery involves cutting slits in the ends of the tubes and inserting wood or metal plates, then through-bolting to complete the joint. Another method is to cut U-shaped scallops in the ends of the tubes, allowing them to fit over the round cross-section of adjoining tubes. Paper tubes readily accept mechanical fasteners, like screws and bolts, which makes them easier to work with than some other, more fragile, forms of paper.

HEX STOOL

Hexagons break down into triangles, which is a structurally sound coincidence. Bees figured this out long ago; more recently, paperboard manufacturers and carbon-fiber fabricators have engineered this pattern into load-bearing panels.

The Hex Stool is supremely simple: six triangular columns, folded out of corrugated boxes, form a geometrically pure seat. Quick and cheap to make, these stools are a perfect solution for temporary event seating, impromptu dinners, or birthday parties. For longer-term use, finish the stool with a coat of wax, water-based polyurethane, or enamel paint, and top it with a pillow or foam pad.

MATERIALS

- Six pieces corrugated card-board (double-wall is best), 21" × 18" each
- PVA (white) glue or wheat paste (see page 25 for recipe)
- Twelve ¾" #8 coarse-thread drywall screws
- Twelve #8 washers

TOOLS

- Pencil
- Tape measure
- Straightedge
- Box cutter
- Binder clips or spring clamps
- Phillips screwdriver

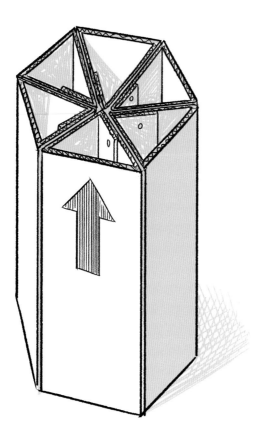

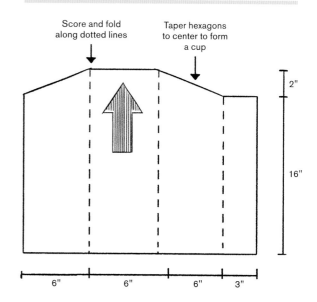

Score and fold along dotted lines

Taper hexagons to center to form a cup

2"

16"

6" 6" 6" 3"

TIP If you're really in a hurry, use three 36" triangular shipping tubes from an office supply store. Cut each in half and binder-clip together.

STEPS

1 **Cut six pieces** of corrugated cardboard as shown above, orienting the grain along the vertical axis. Score lightly along the dotted lines, using the box cutter to slit only through the face paper. Cut all the way through the cardboard along the solid lines. Pay attention to the layout of the template on the cardboard to preserve graphics from the original box for a pop-art touch.

2 **Fold along the scored lines,** overlapping the 3" panel with the first 6" panel to form a triangular column. Glue the 3" flap to the 6" panel and clamp with binder clips, or pin the pieces together with screws, zip ties, rivets, or machine bolts. Repeat to create the five remaining triangles. Let the glue dry.

3 **Clamp the six columns together,** forming a hexagon when viewed from above. The center of the stool should be lower than the outside rim, forming an ergonomic cup shape. Secure each column to the next with two drywall screws, one at the top and one at the bottom, each fitted with a washer under the head. Use a regular (non-powered) screwdriver to prevent blowing through the material. Alternatively, you can use zip ties, pop rivets, binder clips, or glue.

DISPOSAL *Remove the screws. Break the columns into flat pieces and recycle, cut into strips for use as mulch or compost, or use as tinder for the fireplace.*

CUBE
LAMP

Corrugated cardboard is a solid material that is composed of negative space — the long, narrow flutes that create structure also hold a lot of air. Cutting across the grain opens these voids, allowing light to pass through.

The Cube Lamp exploits these properties, laminating squares of corrugated board to create half of a cube, excavated in the center to cradle a modified light fixture. Coat-hanger legs elevate the pile and provide space for the switch and cord. If you have access to a laser cutter, this design is easily adapted to mass production. The laser will also create perfectly clean-cut edges, making for sharp fluted shadows.

MATERIALS

- Double-wall (preferred) or single-wall corrugated cardboard
- PVA glue, wheat paste (see page 25), or rubber cement
- One 6" aluminum studio lamp (see step 4)
- One CFL or LED light bulb, 60W equivalent
- One wire coat hanger

TOOLS

- Pencil
- Ruler
- Box cutter
- Straightedge
- Compass
- Heavy-duty scissors
- Wire snips
- Pliers

CARDBOARD CUTTING TEMPLATE

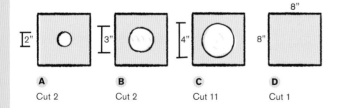

A	B	C	D
Cut 2	Cut 2	Cut 11	Cut 1

STEPS

1 **Cut 16 pieces of cardboard** 8" square with a box cutter and straightedge; use a fresh blade to prevent fuzzy edges.

Note: *If using single-wall cardboard, cut 32 pieces and double the quantities specified at left.*

2 **Separate the squares** into two stacks of eight pieces each. The bottom half of the lamp will have two pieces with a 2" hole (**A**), two with a 3" hole (**B**), and four with a 4" hole (**C**). The

Marking Centerpoints

Mark the precise center of a square or rectangle by setting a straightedge diagonally from corner to corner and drawing a short line along the center of the workpiece. Repeat with the other opposing corners. The intersection of lines is the centerpoint.

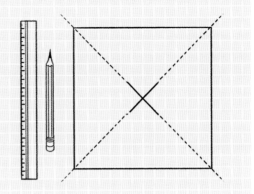

top half will have seven pieces with a 4" hole (**C**) and one solid piece (**D**). Mark the center of each square that gets a hole (see Marking Centerpoints, above), then draw the appropriately sized circle, using a compass. Make the cutouts with the box cutter.

3 **Laminate the pieces** to create each stack, using wheat paste or rubber cement and alternating the direction of the flutes in each layer. Weight down the stacks with books while the glue dries, making sure the layers are aligned. The completed bottom half should have a conical void in the center, while the top half should have a cylindrical void with a solid top.

4 **A standard studio lamp** from the hardware store consists of a conical aluminum shade and plastic socket, attached to a spring clamp. Remove the clamp and cut down the shade with heavy-duty scissors until the lamp nestles down into the bottom half of the bottom cardboard stack. Install the light bulb in the lamp.

Note: *Use compact fluorescent (CFL) or LED light bulbs only! Standard incandescent bulbs can get hot enough to ignite cardboard.*

5 **Cut and straighten** two pieces of coat-hanger wire, each 21" long. Bend each piece into a U shape with three equal 7" arms. Position the top cardboard stack on the bottom unit, then pin the two stacks together by pushing the coat-hanger pieces into the cardboard at right angles

to each other. To change the bulb in the future, gently pull the top half of the lamp off of the coat-hanger pins.

DISPOSAL *Recycle the cardboard halves, coat-hanger metal, and aluminum shade. Remove the light socket for future reuse.*

SIDE VIEW CUTAWAY

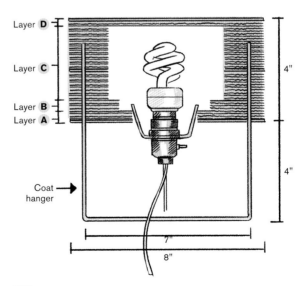

Layer **D**
Layer **C**
Layer **B**
Layer **A**
Coat hanger
4"
4"
7"
8"

TIP This lamp can be converted to a pendant by trimming the leg "pins" to 3", pushing them in all the way, and hanging it upside down by the cord.

BOOK TABLE

Some years ago, a popular TV show birthed a remarkably durable meme: a coffee-table book about coffee tables. Deep in the discount section of a big-box bookstore, I found a book big enough to be a table and envisioned a coffee table made out of a coffee-table book.

The Book Table evolved into an end table, ready to receive the most literary of cocktails. Bolted only through the back cover, the book still functions, allowing guests to flip through a collection of skyscrapers. Build a pair, and bookend the couch, providing some intellectual counterbalance to the TV.

MATERIALS

- One coffee-table book, approximately 18" × 24" (see step 1)
- Four pieces ¾" plywood, 3" × 22"
- Two yellow pine rails, 1½" × 1½" × 22"
- Four ¾" plywood cross-pieces (see diagram on page 37)
- Wood glue
- Finish of your choice
- Four ¼" × 2½" machine bolts
- Four ¼" nuts and washers
- Two ½" × 18" threaded rods
- Eight ½" nuts and washers
- Six 1½" coarse-thread drywall screws
- Six #8 washers

TOOLS

- Pencil
- Tape measure
- Circular saw or table saw
- Miter saw
- Clamps
- Chisel
- Hacksaw
- Drill/driver and ¼" and ½" bits
- Orbital sander or sandpaper, 100- and 120-grit

STEPS

1 **Dimensions shown** are based on an 18" × 24" book. Yours can be larger or as small as 12" × 16"; adjust accordingly to fit your own book. Rip the plywood to width, as shown on facing page, using a table saw or circular saw, then cut the legs to 20" on the miter saw. Miter each end of the legs, in parallel, at 15 degrees, removing as little material as possible. Hold the legs together in a stack to make sure they are the same exact length — this will ensure the table doesn't rock. Use a straight-edge and pencil to measure and mark the tapers on the legs, then cut with a circular saw.

2 **Mark the notches** onto the four plywood cross-pieces, measuring from the center out to ensure a symmetrical structure. Clamp all four pieces together so that the notch markings line up. Set the circular saw blade depth to 1½", then cut through the notches over and over, right next to one another, as shown below. Clean out chips with a chisel. Mark and cut the tapers on the crosspieces. Sand all pieces.

3 **Sandwich each set of legs** between two cross-pieces with a thin, even coat of wood glue, making sure the tops of the legs are flush with the tops of the crosspieces. Clamp together and stand them up, and confirm the leg assembly sits evenly on the ground. Drill through the center of each leg-crosspiece intersection and bolt together, using ¼" bolts and washers on both sides. If desired, countersink the washers and nuts on the outsides of the crosspieces.

4 **Lay the rails into the notches** of the cross-pieces, spacing the leg assemblies 12½" apart,

NOTCHING CROSSPIECES

Clamp crosspieces flush together and make a series of closely spaced, 1½"-deep kerf cuts to create notches for the rails.

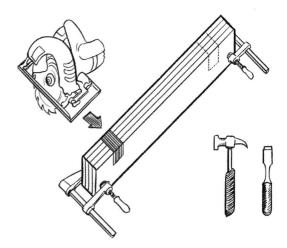

inside-to-inside. Glue the rails down into the crosspieces, then predrill and fasten with drywall screws. Add two coats of finish, if desired.

5 Drill a ½" hole in each leg, 2" up from the bottom end. Cut the threaded rods to length at 16", and insert through the holes in the legs. Use nuts and washers to adjust the legs until the structure is square and straight.

6 Center the book on the structure, then predrill and screw through the back cover, using #8 washers to prevent tear-through.

DISPOSAL *Unscrew the book from the leg assembly and donate to a thrift store or recycle. Remove the threaded rods and recycle. Unbolt and break down the structure – the plywood must be trashed, due to toxic glue, but the rails could be composted or mulched if they have a natural finish.*

CUT LIST

RAIL (Cut 2)

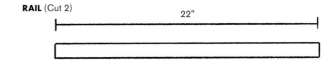

22"

LEG (Cut 4)

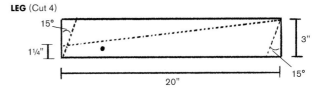

15°   3"

1¼"   20"   15°

CROSSPIECE (Cut 4)

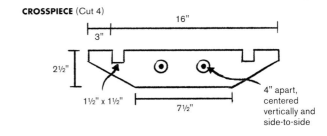

16"
3"
2½"
1½" x 1½"   7½"
4" apart, centered vertically and side-to-side

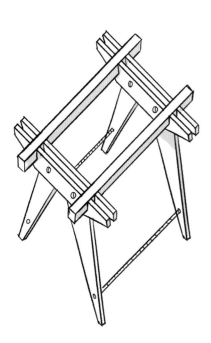

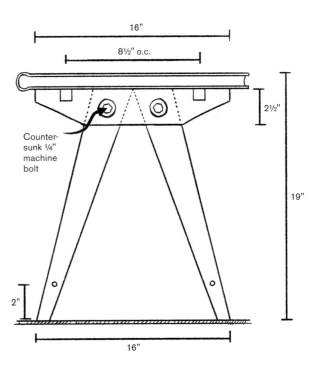

16"
8½" o.c.
2½"
Counter-sunk ¼" machine bolt
19"
2"
16"

CARDBOARD TUBE SCREENS

Folks love living in lofts and working in open-plan offices. The barrier-free lifestyle has its advantages; however, sometimes a fella just needs a little privacy. When I lived in a loft apartment in Alabama, I salvaged a pile of heavy-walled (approximately 3⁄16"-thick) cardboard tubes from the centers of rolls of plotter paper and made screens to section off the bedroom.

The screens are made with tubes suspended horizontally inside wooden frames, creating panels of varying transparency. Joined with some scavenged door hinges, the panels are self-supporting. In my case, six panels, totaling over 18 linear feet, were enough to wall off the bedroom within the loft. The spaces between tubes make for a convenient clothes-drying rack and impromptu closet.

MATERIALS (PER SCREEN)

- Four 6-foot 2×4s, "select" or "prime" grade
- Twenty cardboard tubes, approximately 2½" diameter × 36" long
- Wood glue
- One 1-pound box 1¼" drywall screws
- Sandpaper
- Three heavy-duty door hinges

TOOLS

- Pencil
- Tape measure
- Speed Square
- Drill (corded, heavy-duty drill recommended)
- 2½" hole saw (must match cardboard tube diameter)
- Mallet
- Clamps (optional)
- Countersink bit
- Impact driver

STEPS

1 **Lay out two** of the 2×4 pieces of lumber. Mark the centerlines, lengthwise, on each piece by running a Speed Square down the side of the board with a pencil held on the 1¾" mark. Mark the centers of each tube socket along the centerlines. You can space the tubes (eight per panel) as desired; just make sure to leave at least ¾" between tubes (3¼" on center for 2½" dia. tubes), as closer spacing might split the wood. Using higher-grade lumber ("select" or "prime") for the uprights will also help prevent splitting. For a privacy screen, concentrate the maximum density of tubes between 26" and 54" from the ground. Repeat for a second pair of 2×4s, changing the pattern if desired. See Cut List opposite.

2 **Drill out each center mark** with the hole saw (see below). Put the 2×4 on a sacrificial surface to protect the hole saw and prevent tearout on the backside of the 2×4. Another strategy to prevent tearout is to drill halfway through from one side, until the center mandrel bit just penetrates the back side of the wood, then flip and drill the rest of the material out of all the holes from the back side. Using a hole saw can strain even powerful drills, so take care to let the drill and bit cool down periodically.

3 **Sand the edges** of the holes, removing rough edges and lightly beveling the edges to help the tubes seat (it's a very tight fit).

4 **Assemble each screen panel** by laying one 2×4 upright flat on the ground. Put a little wood glue in each socket and insert the end of the tube, using a mallet and a block to persuade the stubborn ones. Once all the tubes are socketed into one side, put glue on the free ends of the tubes and put the matching upright on top, hammering it into place until all the tubes are firmly seated into the sockets on the top board. A second set of hands is very helpful here, as each tube seems to have a mind of its own.

5 **Clamp the boards to one another,** if necessary, to draw them together and seat the tubes. Pin the tubes to the frame with screws (one in every other tube is fine) through the narrow edge of the uprights and into the sidewalls of the tubes, again predrilling and going slowly to prevent splitting. Let the glue dry completely.

6 **Join the panels** with three hinges, following the spacing shown at right.

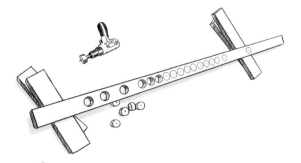

UPRIGHTS Use a corded drill and a hole saw to bore out the uprights. Drill halfway through from one side, until the center mandrel bit just breaks through, then flip the board, re-center the bit, and complete the hole.

> **DISPOSAL** *Remove the screws that connect the tubes to the uprights and use a hammer to break the glue bond, separating the tubes from the uprights. Recycle the tubes. Mulch, compost, burn, or recycle the wood.*

CUT LIST

Twenty 36" cardboard tubes

Two 6' 2x4 uprights for **A**

Two 6' 2x4 uprights for **B**

SIDE VIEW

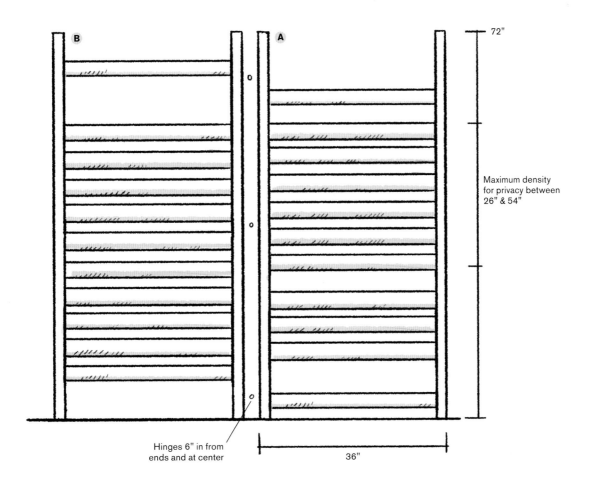

72"

Maximum density
for privacy between
26" & 54"

Hinges 6" in from
ends and at center

36"

STEPS

1 **Cut enough 30" squares** of cardboard to make a stack 5" tall (approximately 40 single-wall sheets). You can piece together smaller sheets, but keep this to a minimum for maximum strength; sandwich any pieced layers between two continuous sheets. Creases are okay, but make sure they are oriented at right angles to one another in adjoining layers for strength.

2 **Lay out two 30"-square pieces** of hardboard on the floor with the rough sides facing up. Brush the rough sides thoroughly with wheat paste (recipe on page 25), making sure to saturate the entire surface. Lay a piece of cardboard on top

of one piece of hardboard. Paint the cardboard with wheat paste, and stack a second piece of cardboard with the grain (corrugation flutes) oriented perpendicular to that of the first piece. Repeat until the stack is 2½" thick, with every layer of corrugation alternated.

Note: *It's important to work as quickly as possible to prevent the glue from drying and/or the cardboard curling from the moisture in the glue before the stack is under clamping pressure.*

Cap the stack with the second piece of hardboard — smooth side facing out — and a piece of plywood to distribute the clamping weight. Evenly lay out plate weights, sandbags, cinderblocks, or other heavy objects on top of the stack. Let the paste cure for at least 24 hours. This is important, as it takes a long time for the center of the laminated stack to dry, and cutting into soggy cardboard will ruin the lamination. Turn a fan on the stack to promote airflow (I have had stacks take so long to dry that they began to mold). Repeat the process to create a second stack.

3 **Lay out the chair silhouette** on the dry stacks as shown at right. Cut out as much as possible with a circular saw, then use a jigsaw to finish up the interior cuts. Cutting laminated cardboard in this way throws up a lot of super-fine dust, so wear a mask and cut in a well-ventilated area.

4 **Lay out the holes for the tubes** according to step 6 of the layout sequence at right. Bore recesses for the tubes with a hole saw, being careful to drill only halfway through the depth of the side pieces.

Note: *Make sure the center mandrel bit of the hole saw will not penetrate the outer hardboard layer.*

The sides with holes should be mirror images of each other. The hole saw will leave a plug behind after it is withdrawn; pry this out with a box cutter.

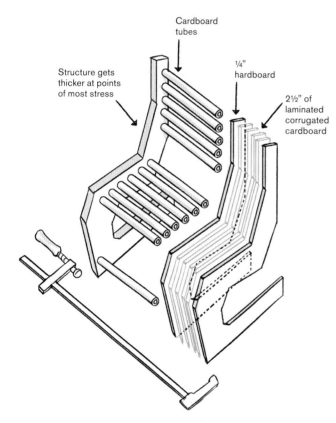

Cardboard tubes

Structure gets thicker at points of most stress

¼" hardboard

2½" of laminated corrugated cardboard

STRUCTURE The hybrid hardboard-corrugated cardboard is a strong, versatile guerilla material. The basic strategy in this chair — bridging two parallel load-bearing frames — can be adapted to a variety of designs.

LAYOUT SEQUENCE

The geometry for the side profile of the cardboard cantilever is a bit tricky. Draw the dotted lines as shown in each numbered step. Solid lines are from previous steps.

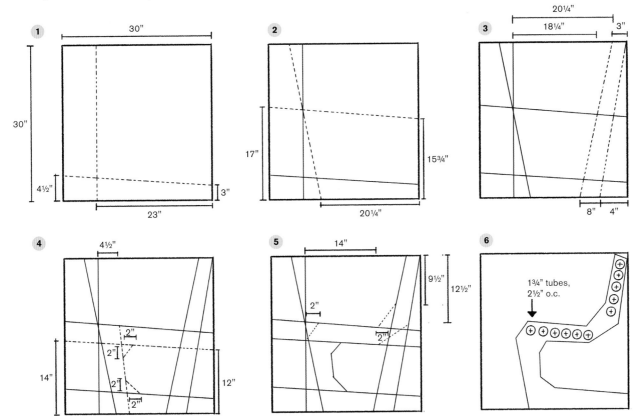

5 **Glue the tubes** into one side with PVA glue, seating the tubes fully into the recesses with a mallet, as needed. Repeat to add the other side. Set the seat up and twist the sides until everything is neat and even and the chair sits squarely on the ground. If necessary, clamp everything together to draw the sides tight. Let the glue dry.

6 **Finish the chair** as desired. Water- or oil-based polyurethane or a simple wax are good options for these materials.

DISPOSAL *If finished without wax, this whole chair can be tossed in a recycling bin, or chopped into pieces and composted.*

CARDBOARD SHELL CHAIR

MATERIALS
- Six 18" pieces 2×6 lumber
- Two pieces 1/8"-thick hard-board, 18" × 18"
- Four 2×4 scraps, at least 18" long
- Wood glue
- 1½" drywall screws
- Wax paper
- Eight pieces single-wall corrugated cardboard, 16" × 16"
- Four pieces single-wall corrugated cardboard, 12" × 16"
- Two strips 1/8" hardboard, 2" × 16"
- Wheat paste (see page 25)
- Polyurethane, wax, or other finish of your choice
- Found chair frame

TOOLS
- Drill/driver
- String (approximately 5 feet long)
- Tape measure
- Pencil
- Paintbrush
- Box cutter
- Six to eight bar clamps, 12" minimum
- Circular saw
- Jigsaw or band saw

Charles and Ray Eames began experimenting with bent plywood during World War II, forcing thin veneers of wood into curving molds under great heat and pressure. Once cured, the resultant forms were light and resilient, making extremely stingy use of material during lean times. Their first product was a leg splint for the war effort, followed by some of the most recognizable chairs of the twentieth century.

The Cardboard Shell Chair manipulates cardboard sheets in the same way, laminating them in curved forms to produce thin, prestressed shells. The curve of the shells, combined with the cross-grain structure of alternating sheets, produces a strong, resilient panel. All you need is a simple mold, six bar clamps, and a pile of salvaged boxes. The shells make great seats and chair backs, and they can be mounted to a new or salvaged chair frame. This case study describes the construction of a single 16"-square shell; you can modify this as needed to fit any chair frame.

STEPS

1. **Pop a screw** into the top of your workbench. Tie one end of the string to the screw, and tie the other end to a pencil; when pulled taut, the pencil should be 48" from the screw. Using this apparatus as a compass, mark a 48" radius on each chunk of 2×6, making sure the radius is centered left-to-right and top-to-bottom on each piece of wood, as shown at right.

2. **Cut the marked curves** with a jigsaw or band saw, creating three positive (convex) curved ribs and three negative (concave) curved ribs that fit together.

3. **Screw and glue the ribs** to two 18" squares of hardboard, with one rib at each end and one in the middle; start at one edge of the sheet and work toward the middle and opposite edge, letting the hardboard gradually conform to the curve. Screw scraps of 2×4 along the ends of the ribs to connect them and add some stiffness to the mold structure. You should now have two halves of a mold that nestle together, as shown at right.

4. **Lay a sheet of wax paper** in the mold to prevent the wheat paste from gluing the mold shut. Lay one 16" square of corrugated cardboard in the

concave mold and coat thoroughly with wheat paste. Layer a second piece of cardboard, turning the direction of the corrugations (flutes) perpendicular to the first. When the corrugations run opposite to the curve of the mold, score the cardboard lightly (cutting only through the facing) with a box cutter across the corrugations to help it conform to the curve.

5 **After building up four layers** of 16" pieces, place the 2" × 16" hardboard strips at the side edges and the 12" × 16" cardboard pieces centered between the strips. The hardboard strips create solid areas in the shell that will accept fasteners. Make sure the hardboard is saturated with glue, as its relative denseness sometimes prevents it from sticking well to cardboard.

6 **Add the remaining four 16" square pieces** of cardboard, top with a sheet of wax paper, and cap off the stack with the convex half of the mold. Clamp the mold together along the edges, using a bar clamp at the ends of each 2×6 rib. Tighten all the clamps a little bit at a time, working around until the entire mold is evenly compressed, the cardboard has conformed to the curve, and some wheat paste has squeezed out along the edges. Wipe up the excess wheat paste with a damp rag and allow the assembly to dry for at least 24 hours.

7 **The dried shell** should be stiff and sturdy, with the slightest amount of give to it. Trim the edges of the shell as needed to fit your chair, using a circular saw and a straightedge or a jigsaw for curves.

8 **Make a second shell** for the chair back, as applicable. Mount the shells to your chair frame (found or built from scratch) by screwing through the chair frame and into the hardboard strips at the edges. Finish with wax or water-based polyurethane.

DISPOSAL *Cut into strips and compost, or recycle with paper waste.*

MAKESHIFT COMPASS

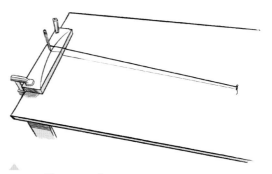

ABOVE Use a pencil, a screw, and some twine to create a makeshift 48"-radius compass.

CARDBOARD SHELL MOLD

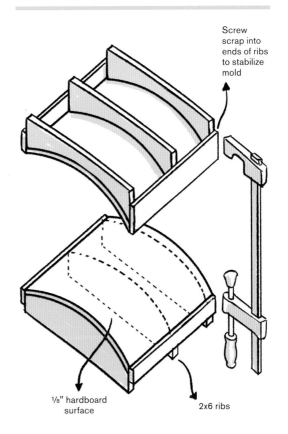

Screw scrap into ends of ribs to stabilize mold

⅛" hardboard surface

2x6 ribs

AMERICA IS A NATION MADE OF WOOD, BUILT ON THE BACK OF A DENSE PRE-COLONIAL FOREST.

Native Americans used fire and selective transplanting of trees to manage tracts of land. Great Plains tribes used grass fires to keep the prairies open and support populations of bison. Once Europeans arrived, with metal tools and draft animals, they wiped the landscape clean, building cabins, fences, and everything else they needed out of the trees they felled when clearing land for agriculture.

Wood construction in the New World began with post-and-beam or whole-log structures. Technological innovations – mechanized nail production and water-powered sawmills – revolutionized construction in the 1840s. Carpenters began to use balloon framing to quickly erect cheap buildings out of standardized, premilled lumber. Long studs ran from the foundation to the eaves, supporting the roof. The building was braced and sheathed by thin planks nailed across the studs, forming a shear diaphragm wall system. After the Civil War, the balloon system evolved into platform framing, where studs only run from floor to floor, allowing for shorter, more efficient stud lengths.

This American way of building birthed cities from coast to coast as the population expanded westward. It also fueled several cataclysmic fires, in San Francisco, Chicago, Baltimore, and Pittsburgh. Despite changing building codes and diminishing forest cover, light wood framing remains the dominant residential construction system in the country. Regional tree plantations and mills, combined with fast rail and trucking networks, can bring standardized, quality lumber to any doorstep in the country. Fasteners, tools, and precut pieces of wood are available at every hardware store. Most lumber sold in America was harvested and milled on the continent, which makes it an in-sourced, (relatively) locavore material. An "FSC" (Forest Stewardship Council) stamp means that a particular wood product meets certain environmental standards in forest management and manufacture. However, as efficient as it is, America's timber infrastructure faces growing competition from tropical clear-cutting and cheap Baltic imports, used heavily in premanufactured products such as IKEA furniture.

Wood is valuable to the guerilla for its ubiquity, workability, durability, and low cost. It is also a raw, elemental material, used by mankind for shelter and heat since the beginning of time. Even the most drab, beige-carpeted garden apartment feels more alive with a natural wood table in the kitchen.

MATERIALS

DIMENSIONAL LUMBER

Dimensional lumber is the standard array of framing timbers for constructing wood-framed buildings. There is a difference between the nominal and the actual measurements of lumber, so that what we call a 2×4 does not actually measure 2" × 4"; it's more like 1½" × 3½". The discrepancy is born out of shrinkage, the milling process, and historical customs.

Most building lumber sold in the South and along the Eastern Seaboard is Southern yellow pine. SYP grows fast and straight, which makes it ideal for plantation-style management. In northern regions of the country, larch, fir, spruce, and white pine dominate. After growing for about 30 years, trees are cut and kiln-dried to a moisture content of around 15 percent. The lumber is then graded for straightness and structural strength. The truest boards with best strength characteristics and fewest knots are stamped "Select," followed by "1," "2," "Stud," "Utility," and "Economy." Most big-box stores don't sell anything below stud grade.

SYP is extremely strong for its weight. It has an unremarkable yellowish grain, often streaked with greens, grays, and blacks. Boards pick up stains and dents easily, and will have numbers and letters stamped on them. Most framing lumber (nominally

Standard Lumber Sizes — Nominal and Actual

NOMINAL SIZE	ACTUAL SIZE
1×3	¾" × 2½"
1×4	¾" × 3½"
1×6	¾" × 5½"
1×8	¾" × 7¼"
1×10	¾" × 9¼"
1×12	¾" × 11¼"
2×4	1½" × 3½"
2×6	1½" × 5½"
2×8	1½" × 7¼"
2×10	1½" × 9¼"
2×12	1½" × 11¼"

2" thick) today is milled with a roundover on the edges and some surfacing to minimize splinters. The quick growing cycle and rapid kiln-drying tend to soften and weaken the grain, making the wood susceptible to splitting and absorbing moisture.

SPECIALTY SOFTWOODS

Specialty softwoods are other light-grained woods besides pine and other standard species. Some are available at the typical big-box store, but most have to be foraged or sourced at a large lumberyard. The guerilla can often find pieces of knot-free pine or poplar in old furniture, cabinets, door casements, or other trim.

Cedar is a beautiful, sweet-smelling wood that is naturally rot-resistant (if you use the heartwood). *Red* cedar has a warm amber color and is sought after for fence posts and other outdoor applications. *White* cedar is light-colored with bold red streaks, and is knottier and more susceptible to splitting. Fine, straight grain and a lack of density translate into easy workability.

Poplar is a homely wood – greenish-yellow with sometimes-prominent green streaks. However, it is tight-grained and dense enough to be dimensionally stable. It's also relatively cheap. These properties make it popular with cabinetmakers, furniture manufacturers, and DIYers for applications where the grain will be hidden under paint or other finishes.

Redwood, though now in dire circumstances in the wild, was once used widely for siding and water towers. The spongy grain swells when saturated, making the wood perfect for building a watertight barrel. Water towers, once common on top of urban buildings and in railroad yards, are slowly going extinct. Redwood (and its water-tower cousin, cypress) can be found in architectural salvage yards. Very soft, and light for its size, redwood is not the best structural lumber, but is gorgeous, uniformly grained, and generally free of knots.

HARDWOOD

Hardwood has long been preferred by furniture makers for its superior strength. America was once lousy with hardwood trees such as oak, maple, and hickory, but overharvesting and a long growing cycle have made hardwoods more and more expensive. All hardwoods are harder to work with, as their tighter grain puts more strain on blades and bits.

Oak is one of the most common hardwoods. It is extremely hard and dense, with a handsome, if monotonous, grain structure. Light gold in color, it looks good with a clearcoat or a darkening stain. Commonly used in flooring and furniture of all kinds, its ubiquity makes it one of the cheaper hardwoods.

Maple is a truly American hardwood, growing in the north part of the continent. It has a super-fine grain, which can look like a chain of small ellipses. Maple's fine grain and lack of porosity make it a favored material for butcher-block countertops and cutting boards. That same density also makes it very "burny" on the saw, so use a fresh, high-tooth-count blade for clean cuts.

Ash, an American relative of the olive tree, is hard yet resilient, favored for baseball bats and tool handles. That resiliency, coupled with a straight grain, makes ash a good candidate for bending applications and furniture construction. It is indigenous to all of the continent east of the Mississippi, and some parts west, where it has fallen prey to the invasive emerald ash borer. As a result, inexpensive salvage-logged ash may be available in certain regions.

Hickory (and pecan, a subspecies) is an indigenous American hardwood, light in color and super-tight-grained. Known for resilience, hickory is used to make hammer handles and drumsticks and for smoking meat. Common in the American South, it is excellent for chair parts and other high-strength applications.

Walnut is a cocoa-colored wood with a straight grain and high oil content, which gives off a peculiar odor when cut. Much like other hardwoods, it is strong and dense, favored for bookcases, architectural millwork, gunstocks, and flooring. The cheapest source is usually flooring. Look for flooring seconds, which will have knots and other defects that lower the price significantly.

PLYWOOD

Modern plywood was invented in Portland, Oregon, in 1905. The Portland Manufacturing Company, which made wooden boxes, prototyped a process for creating sheet goods out of cross-laminated veneers of Douglas fir. By the 1920s, plywood was used for car parts and in door production. In World War II, plywood was used to make patrol boats and gliders. In the postwar housing boom, sheet goods revolutionized construction by replacing planks in sheathing, subfloor, and roofing applications. Houses could go up much faster, and the resultant wall systems were stronger and less susceptible to seasonal swelling and shrinking.

Plywood is now used extensively in residential construction; panel production in cabinets and case-work; concrete formwork; and in specialty furniture. The grain of each sheet of veneer is turned perpendicular to the adjacent sheets, creating a strong, split- and twist-resistant panel. It's commonly sold in 4 × 8-foot sheets, in thicknesses from ⅛" to ¾". Much like stud lumber, plywood sheets are graded:

- **"A" surfaces** *are free of defects. The wood may be clear (no knots or repairs) or the knots may have been cut out, replaced with football-shaped patches, and sanded in. Gaps in the edges are filled with putty.*
- **"B" surfaces** *are patched and sanded.*
- **"C" and "D" surfaces** *may have significant defects, but the panels are guaranteed to be well-glued.*

Baltic birch plywood is usually imported from Northern Europe or Russia. It is extremely uniform, with a fine pale grain and no defects. The expense and non-local origins make it a poor choice for the guerilla, but it does look nice!

Bamboo plywood is made from oriented, compressed strands of bamboo fiber. One or two manufacturers produce it in America, but the vast majority is made in China and shipped around the world. It is strong, heavy, and made from a rapidly renewable resource, but it is very expensive and has a large carbon footprint.

Hardwood veneer plywood is used for fine cabinetry when solid wood is too expensive. The outer veneers are a thin skin of hardwood, with a core of MDF (see below) or plywood. These plywoods look nice, but are expensive and reveal their true nature along their cut edges. Professional cabinetry shops add a thin strip of veneer, called edge-banding, to the cut edges to cover up the cheap core material.

OSB, or oriented strand board, is similar to plywood but looks like compressed mulch. It is made with wood chips and sawdust, saturated in glue and laminated under high pressure. The resultant board is cheap, and often used for sheathing or subflooring. However, it lacks the continuous grain structure of alternating veneers, which makes it weak.

MDF, or medium density fiberboard, has been around since the 1980s. It is made from lumber-mill residuals and sawdust, bound together with resin and wax. The resultant sheets are uniform, dense and grainless, making them a good choice for cabinets, shelves, boxes, or anything requiring dimensional stability.

PALLET WOOD

Pallets are a key part of the international shipping industry, packaging consumer goods into forklift-friendly units. They can be found all over cities: in dumpsters, on loading docks, and around jobsites. Secondhand pallets sell wholesale for two to four dollars, depending on their condition.

Due to their weight-bearing requirements, pallets are often made of hardwoods — maple, ash, and oak being the most common. Five or more wood planks form the flat top surface and are supported by three internal stringers made of 2×4 or 4×4 lumber. Another two or three planks run across the bottom, keeping the stringers from twisting.

Pallets can be a cheap source of hardwood, but it comes at a steep labor cost. Lower-grade, tight-grained hardwood that has been sitting outside,

TRANSFORMING FOUND FURNITURE — ESPECIALLY THAT PERENNIAL URBAN DANDELION, OLD IKEA FURNITURE — IS AN ART UNTO ITSELF.

absorbing moisture and getting abused by heavy machinery, makes for gnarly boards. The continual swelling and shrinking associated with moisture exposure grabs tight to nails, making them hard to pry apart. Be prepared to sink some time into tearing the wood apart, de-nailing it and milling it into usable pieces.

Pallet wood may be chemically pressure-treated to retard rot or fumigated to prevent bug infestation. Pressure-treated wood can be unusually heavy for its size and often has a yellow-green color, but identification is not always clear. Do not burn pressure-treated wood, or cut without good ventilation, as the chemicals used in treatment are known carcinogens.

SALVAGE AND OLD-GROWTH

Homes built before World War II are likely to contain old-growth lumber, roughly defined as wood that comes from trees that are 80 to 100 years old at time of felling. Current timber production is based on a 20- to 30-year harvesting cycle, making for spongy, looser-grained wood. Old-growth lumber was shade-grown in the wild, a slower process that results in tighter, denser grain. Lumber salvaged from the demolition of old homes has been drying out inside a wall assembly for 50 to 100 years, producing boards that are straight and stable.

Architectural salvage yards are becoming more common in urban areas, selling reclaimed old-growth studs and joists by the foot. Pick through the pile, selecting for straightness. Make sure to de-nail thoroughly, using a stud finder (wall scanner) or metal detector to find any buried fasteners. Be wary of pieces with paint, which is likely to be lead-based. Some purveyors will plane the wood for you, producing at least one clean, beautiful surface. If not planed, use a belt sander to grind off the years. In additional to salvage yards, look for old-growth in dumpsters beside renovation projects, or in the walls of your own property when fixing up the house.

DOORS AND ASSEMBLED OBJECTS

Lots of lumber is available to the guerilla for the price of disassembly. Old doors, windows, and furniture (especially bookshelves) may yield a significant amount of wood when taken apart. Crating, found in the same places as pallets, is usually made of plywood or softwood strips that are easy to harvest. Transforming found furniture — especially that perennial urban dandelion, old IKEA furniture — is an art unto itself. Old sofas and easy chairs may yield handsome turned legs or feet, often made of hardwood. Scour alleys, secondhand shops, and yard sales for likely candidates, taking a drill, Crescent wrench, hammer, and crowbar for field disassembly.

TOOLS

CIRCULAR SAW

The handheld circular saw is the most versatile, yet most inaccurate, of basic cutting tools. Much like a pioneer with an ax, one could build an entire house with nothing but a circular saw. It can cut both with the grain of wood (called *ripping*) and across the grain (*crosscutting*), and can easily handle plywood and other sheet goods. The tool consists of a motor and a round blade, housed in a lightweight body with a spring-loaded blade guard and pistol grip.

Cutting a straight line with a circular saw takes practice. Much like driving, it helps to focus your eye a little ahead of the blade instead of right at the cut point. For super-accurate cuts, use an edge guide (some saws come with them) to ride along the edge of the material being cut. Alternatively, clamp down a carpenter's level or a straight board and ride the edge of the saw's baseplate against the fence.

When shopping for a new circular saw, look for a lightweight, 15- to 20-amp saw with an adjustable baseplate — both depth and bevel — and a standard 7¼" blade diameter. Avoid worm-drive saws, which are bigger, heavier, and more expensive than standard ("sidewinder") saws and are made for heavy-duty cutting.

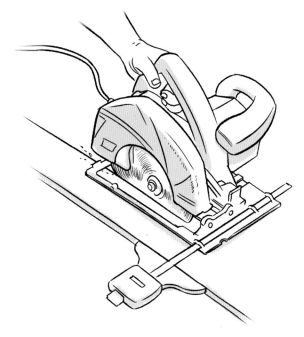

▲ **CIRCULAR SAW WITH EDGE GUIDE.** Use a finishing blade (48–60 teeth) for smooth cuts in plywood. Use a cheaper framing blade (24 teeth) for dimensional lumber.

MITER SAW

Sometimes called a chop saw (but not to be confused with a metal chop saw; see page 152), a miter saw is a precise, stationary circular saw made for crosscuts. It consists of a motor and blade on a spring-loaded arm that moves up and down. Most models these days are compound miter saws, meaning they can make cuts at any angle up to 45 degrees in two axes — both vertically and horizontally. This makes it the ideal machine for cutting coping, baseboards, handrails, crown molding, flooring, and other trim elements that involve a lot of mitering. For building furniture, a miter saw makes it very easy to produce angled legs and tight corners.

Miter saws can be expensive, and not so easy to lug around. Look to borrow one from a neighbor, friend, or contractor. Alternately, most hardware stores will make simple crosscuts for you at the store for a small fee. Big-box stores rent them by the hour; if you plan your cut list, you can get the saw, make your cuts, and get it back to the store at minimal cost.

TABLE SAW

A table saw is basically a big, stable, cast-iron table with an adjustable circular saw mounted inside of it. The blade can be raised and lowered, or tilted up to 45 degrees to make bevel cuts. An adjustable fence slides from side to side, providing a straight guide for running the material against. It is used for ripping cuts. Crosscuts can be made on a table saw, but they require a miter gauge or a sled to support the material and prevent kickback. A contractor table saw is a lightweight, portable version of the stationary shop tool, with a smaller table and a shorter fence; some have folding legs, while others are designed to sit on a tabletop or separate stand. Contractor table saws are about the same price as a good miter saw and are loud, bulky machines. They're also not as accurate as stationary table saws, due to the light weight of their tables (less stable) and the short length of their fences. Instead of buying a table saw, you can borrow some time on one at an established woodshop, makerspace, or school.

JIGSAW

A jigsaw is a handheld saw with a straight, reciprocating blade that moves in a vertical axis. The blade is thin, flexible, and mounted in a chuck that allows some twisting. Jigsaws are made for curving cuts, tight angles, notches, or working small pieces of material that would get kicked

out of a circular saw. Clamp down the workpiece securely, and work slowly, following your cutting line. It may be necessary to make a series of relief cuts, removing small pieces of material one at a time, if the blade can't turn tightly enough to cut out the greater shape all at once.

DRILL/IMPACT DRIVER

In furniture making, nails are rarely used anymore — joints are glued and screwed for maximum strength. A drill is often sold as a multipurpose tool, for drilling holes and driving fasteners. However, a drill is meant to operate at a high speed and low torque, which is bad for driving fasteners. Trying to drive screws with a drill often leads to stripped screws, twisted wrists, and muttered curses. An impact driver — low speed, high torque — is designed solely for driving fasteners. Predrill all your fastener holes to help with alignment, prevent splitting, and reduce stress on the driver.

Buying a drill and driver as a set, typically including two batteries and a charger, is the best way to get both for a reasonable price. Newer models use lithium-ion batteries, reducing weight and recharge times. Always spring for 18-volt models, as smaller drills have little power and terrible battery life. If you get only one tool, go with a ⅜" drill that is light and well-balanced. With practice, you'll learn to use the variable-speed trigger with a light touch to prevent overdriving or stripping screws.

ROUTER

A router is a shaping tool that looks like a squat cylinder with handles. A round bit projects from the bottom, spinning at high speed. There are dozens of different bits for routers, each imparting a particular shape to a material. Most often, they are used for edging — forming a roundover, a chamfer, or coving. They can also be used to make grooves, flush up uneven edges, or carve designs into flat surfaces. Remember that a router is a precision tool for shaping, not cutting. Hogging out a lot of material in one pass quickly burns out expensive bits, not to mention motors and forearms.

Choosing Drill Bits

The standard bit for making holes up to ½" in diameter is the *twist* bit, which has a cutting edge that forms a twisted spiral up the shaft of the bit. For larger holes, *spade* or *paddle* bits, named for their resemblance to those two implements, have a pointed pilot tip and a broad cutting edge that is perpendicular to the shaft of the bit. *Forstner* bits, used in fine woodworking applications, are shaped like upside-down cups (with the cutting edge around the rim) and have no pilot bit. They make clean, flat-bottomed holes but can be very tricky to use, as they do not readily center themselves. *Hole saws*, used for very large-diameter holes, have a central mandrel pilot bit and interchangeable cup-shaped cutters.

If you're using an impact driver in place of a standard drill, keep in mind that impact drivers have a different chuck system that accepts only bits with a knurled, hexagonal end.

SANDERS AND SANDPAPER

All woodwork needs to be sanded and finished at some point. Guerilla furniture, in particular, using salvaged wood, needs surfacing to bring out its beauty and protect the user from splinters. The simplest and cheapest power sander is a quarter-sheet sander, made to accept standard sheets of flat sandpaper that have been torn into quarters. Little wire clamps secure the paper, and the motor vibrates the pad around. Orbital sanders use round sheets, usually backed with Velcro to attach to a vibrating pad. The pad moves in a random, elliptical orbit to prevent a pattern of scratches from appearing. I prefer the quarter-sheet machines because they are cheaper up-front, use cheaper sandpaper, and their square footprint allows for working tight into corners.

Belt sanders are powerful machines that use a continuous band of sandpaper looped around two rollers to abrade the wood. They are great for quickly removing large amounts of material, grinding off old finishes, or smoothing uneven laminated surfaces. However, since the belt moves in a linear direction, it can leave prominent scratch marks, even when working with the grain, and it's very easy for a novice operator to remove too much material or create dips in a surface. Use a belt sander at the preliminary stages of finishing, then move to an orbital or quarter-sheet sander and ascending grits to finish off.

For stripping paint or other finishes and smoothing rough-sawn lumber, start with 80-grit sandpaper; use 100-grit paper for general smoothing, 120-grit for finishing, and 220- to 320-grit for sanding between coats of finish.

METHODS

FASTENER SELECTION AND USE

The modern guerilla does not have to rely on the complex joinery systems used in traditional woodworking: he has a vast array of mechanical fasteners available at the local hardware store. However, each type of wood and project requires careful fastener selection for the best strength, appearance, and durability.

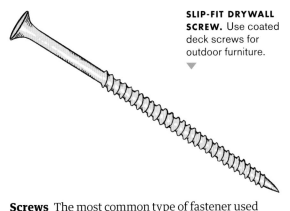

SLIP-FIT DRYWALL SCREW. Use coated deck screws for outdoor furniture.

Screws The most common type of fastener used in cabinetry and furniture construction is the #8 coarse-thread drywall screw. Cheap, dependable, and readily available, drywall screws come in lengths from ¾" to 3". Standard versions have a black finish and Phillips-drive head, but professional cabinetmakers prefer square-headed screws because they resist stripping and look neater. At lengths of 1½" and up, these screws are slip-fit fasteners: the bottom two-thirds of the shaft of the screw is threaded, while the top one-third is smooth, at a smaller diameter than the threaded portion. This allows the top portion to slide freely through the first piece of material, while the threads grip the second piece of material, drawing the two tightly together. Avoid so-called "wood screws" that are threaded all the way to the underside of the head, as they can actually drive pieces of wood apart.

Drill pilot holes (or "predrill") for #8 screws with a ⅛"-diameter bit, set to a depth about ¼" shorter than the length of the fastener. An adjustable countersink bit will also bore a shallow cone that allows the screw head to sit flush with the top surface of the wood. Predrilling is especially important in hardwoods, as they are brittle and vulnerable to splitting. For anything that will be outside or exposed to moisture, use galvanized or stainless-steel #8 deck screws instead of drywall screws.

Coarse-thread drywall screws are a bit thick for fastening into the edges of plywood, tending to split the plies. I like the Spax fasteners designed for going into the end-grain of plywood. The lead threads have burrs that cut into the wood, eliminating the need for predrilling and preventing splitting. The head recess is a star shape, which is very resistant to stripping.

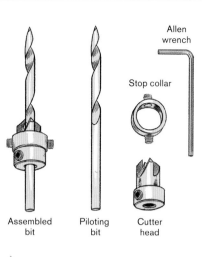

SPAX SCREW. Use for fastening into the edge grain in plywood.

ADJUSTABLE COUNTERSINK BIT. A movable cutter head bores a shallow cone that allows screw heads to lie flush.

LAG BOLT. Use for structural and de-mountable joints.

THREADED SOCKET. Use for bolt-together, flat-pack designs.

Bolts Several projects in this section use *lag bolts* or *through-bolts*. Lag bolts are oversize screws, with hex heads that you drive with a ratchet wrench and socket. These fasteners are used in heavy structural applications, like deck and stair construction, making them good for constructing strong joints in large pieces, such as tables and beds. A simple ratchet-head accessory for an impact driver makes driving lags much easier. To make flat-pack joints, use threaded sockets (also known as insert nuts) — metal tubes with interior threading and barbs on the outside. Buried in the receiving piece of wood, they accept fasteners through repeated assembly and disassembly without stripping the joint.

A through-bolt is any standard blunt-ended bolt, such as a machine bolt or carriage bolt, that goes fully through two pieces of material and accepts a nut, squeezing the two pieces together. Through-bolting is one of the strongest ways to join two pieces of wood and typically is used in constructing decks, balconies, stairs, and cantilevered framing. Use washers under the head of the bolt and the nut to distribute pressure on the wood, and take care not to overtighten, to prevent crushing the washer into the wood grain.

Many of the flat-pack pieces in this section have their fasteners exposed. It is imperative to lay out the holes neatly and drill counterbores to sink the bolt heads flush, which will give a clean, finished appearance. Where disassembly is not a priority, screws can be hidden by counterboring and plugging: drill a ¼"- or ⅜"-diameter hole about ¼" deep for the counterbore, then drill a smaller pilot hole for the screw and drive the screw. Plug the hole with a short section of dowel and some glue. Plug-cutters — drill bits that cut out little buttons of wood — can be used to create plugs that match the material of the piece exactly.

Glue Glue is an essential partner to screws and other fasteners. Standard yellow wood glue penetrates the grain structures of adjoining pieces of wood, forming bonds across them. If tightly clamped and properly cured, the resultant joint will be stronger than the wood itself. The more surface area available for bonding, the stronger the joint; simple notching, dadoing, or rabbeting will multiply the area for the glue to grab and exponentially increase strength.

Grain orientation also affects the strength of a glue bond. End-grain (the surface exposed when you cut across the grain of a piece of lumber) is like a bundle of straws — the grain structure will wick the glue away from the surface of the joint, preventing a proper bond. Avoid gluing into end-grain whenever possible. Gluing surfaces parallel to the grain creates a much stronger bond. If you're using salvaged wood, make sure that any previously applied paint, varnish, or other finish is removed, as they will also interfere with bonding.

Regular yellow glue is great for the majority of applications, but some types of wood and higher-strength applications call for a polyurethane glue (e.g., Gorilla glue). Polyurethane glue is brown and extremely sticky, and it stains skin and other surfaces. It cures in the presence of moisture, meaning the wood must be dampened with water (or used with yellow glue, for a hybrid bond) before the glue is applied. Then the pieces must be clamped very tightly. As it cures, polyurethane glue expands, which can push your joint apart. Yellow foam will bubble out of the joint and harden, at which point it can be scraped away. Use polyurethane glue sparingly to avoid excessive squeeze-out and expansion.

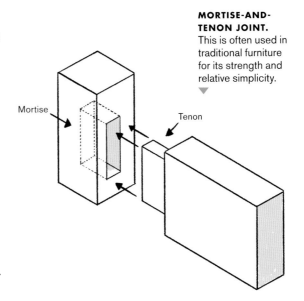

MORTISE-AND-TENON JOINT. This is often used in traditional furniture for its strength and relative simplicity.

Mortise

Tenon

TENONING

Mortise-and-tenon joinery is one of the oldest construction techniques. It consists of a tenon, or projection, and a matching mortise, or recess. Old barns and houses, built with post-and-beam frames, are often held together with nothing but mortise-and-tenon joinery and greenwood pegs.

Tenoning is a great technique for high-strength applications, such as joining table legs to tops. Mark out the mortise first, making sure to keep the corners tight and square. Drill slightly inside the mark at each of the four corners, using a ½" bit. Using those as entry holes, use a jigsaw to cut out the mortise, again staying slightly inside the marks. Finish the joint to size by carefully paring away excess material with a sharp chisel. Avoid using a hammer with the chisel; if it doesn't shave cleanly with hand pressure, it isn't sharp enough. Match the tenon the same way, cutting it slightly large with a jigsaw, then test-fitting and sizing with a chisel.

PLYWOOD JOINERY

Plywood is a powerful innovation, freeing the guerilla from the tyranny of planks and allowing for large, flat, smooth surfaces with a minimum of work. However, the laminated plies make plywood liable to split along the edge — from fasteners, moisture, or shoddy gluing at the factory. Plywood also can be floppy, and even ¾" material often needs some sort of rib to stiffen the structure.

Plywood works best in perpendicular orientations — a box, for instance, where each of the five sides serves to brace the others and prevent flexing. This logic can be applied to any plywood piece. T- and L-shaped cross-sections, where one piece is screwed through the flat side and into the edge of the mating piece, create strong, braced frames. For tabletops, box out a flat sheet with thin strips of plywood or dimensional lumber around the underside, forming an *apron* (see page 17).

LAMINATION

Lamination refers to the gluing together of multiple pieces of lumber to create a bigger piece, usually a broad surface, like a tabletop. The key to good glue-ups is surfacing. The boards to be joined must be square and straight. Professional shops use a jointer and a planer to clean up the wood. Absent pro tools, a board can be hand-jointed by snapping a chalk line along the wild edge and then hand-planing it straight or carefully cutting with a circular saw. If you have access to a table saw, boards can be reasonably straightened by cutting ¼" off one side edge, flipping the board, cutting ¼" off the other side, and repeating as necessary. The flipping and recutting help to average out the board's irregularities.

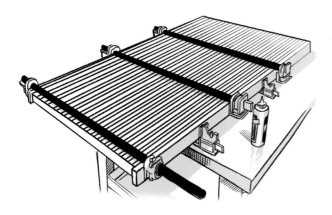

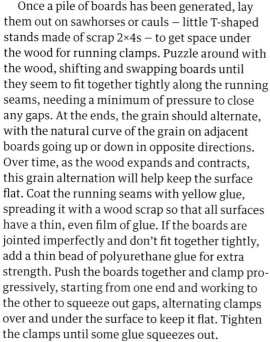

▲
CLAMPS. Alternate clamps over and under the assembly to prevent bowing. You can buy pipe clamp heads for a reasonable price; mate them with scrap pipe.

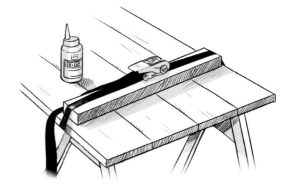

▲
RATCHET STRAPS. You can use ratchet straps in lieu of long clamps, but they have a tendency to bow the assembly. A crosswise board under the ratchet straps helps counteract bowing.

Once a pile of boards has been generated, lay them out on sawhorses or cauls — little T-shaped stands made of scrap 2×4s — to get space under the wood for running clamps. Puzzle around with the wood, shifting and swapping boards until they seem to fit together tightly along the running seams, needing a minimum of pressure to close any gaps. At the ends, the grain should alternate, with the natural curve of the grain on adjacent boards going up or down in opposite directions. Over time, as the wood expands and contracts, this grain alternation will help keep the surface flat. Coat the running seams with yellow glue, spreading it with a wood scrap so that all surfaces have a thin, even film of glue. If the boards are jointed imperfectly and don't fit together tightly, add a thin bead of polyurethane glue for extra strength. Push the boards together and clamp progressively, starting from one end and working to the other to squeeze out gaps, alternating clamps over and under the surface to keep it flat. Tighten the clamps until some glue squeezes out.

Lacking clamps, use ratchet straps. Put some wax paper between the strap and the surface so the straps don't get glued to the wood. If laminating on the wide edge (so that the assembly of narrow edges becomes the finished surface), dispense with clamps altogether and screw each layer to the one previous. Check with a carpenter's square to maintain a

flat top surface. In conjunction with screws, bore a set of holes through each board that all match up, layer to layer, and push ½"-diameter threaded rods through the entire assembly, then ratchet down the rods tightly (see page 97). For a mechanical (no glue) lamination, lay out all the boards next to one another, set a circular saw to a ½" depth, and cut two parallel dadoes, 2" wide, across the underside of the assembly. Fit in 2"-wide strips of ½" plywood and glue and screw into each board.

GUERILLA FINISHING

Wood finishing is an art form . . . and it can spiral into a rabbit hole of ever-deeper complexity. Professional shops use spray-finishing, requiring a ventilated booth, high-test lacquer, and an air compressor. This results in a clean, smooth, texture-free surface. However, it is toxic and requires some heavy-duty equipment. The projects in this section focus on low-effort, nontoxic, off-the-shelf finishes.

Mineral oil is the go-to first stop for the guerilla. It is available at drugstores as a stomach remedy (it's so nontoxic it's edible) and costs very little. Applied to wood with a rag, then wiped off after a few minutes, it provides a clear, low-gloss finish, perfect for projects that will contact food, like cutting boards. Warming it slightly in the microwave can aid penetration into the wood. Periodic re-oiling is necessary, especially if the surface gets wet often. Mineral oil doesn't really change the color of the wood or bring out the grain.

Tung oil is made from the seeds of the nuts of the tung tree, which grows in Asia. In its natural state, it is edible and nontoxic. However, it is typically polymerized — heated to a high temperature to increase viscosity — and mixed with thinners and driers, typically petroleum-based, to make it more workable. Look for a tung oil that explicitly says it only uses citrus-based thinners, or is 100 percent pure. Cut pure tung oil with turpentine to achieve a workable consistency. Apply it with a clean, lint-free rag, and allow it to penetrate for a few minutes, then buff it off. It will condition, improve water resistance, and add a warm glow to wood of all types.

Linseed oil is pressed from flax seeds and is used as a nutritional supplement in its raw state. For woodworking, it is polymerized by boiling, which renders it inedible. Like all oils, it soaks in and conditions wood, restoring a small measure of natural balance to the grain. However, linseed oil is not the most water-resistant finish and can darken light woods considerably. It is typically cut with paint thinner by at least a quarter to facilitate penetration. Apply it using the same technique as with other oils, wetting on and buffing off after allowing it to penetrate. Make sure to buff off thoroughly, or the oil will dry in a gummy buildup that cannot be removed without turpentine or thinner.

Polyurethane is a complex chemical product, made of chains of molecules joined by a class of chemicals known as urethanes. It can be made into solid plastics and foams or left liquid as a wood finish. *Oil-based polyurethane* dries to a hard, impervious, amber-colored finish. Apply it with a brush, being careful to avoid drips and runs, and let the finish dry for 6 hours between coats. Oil-based polyurethane is sticky, requiring paint thinner (another toxic solvent) for cleanup, and will yellow significantly if exposed to a lot of sunlight.

Water-based polyurethane is low-toxicity, low-VOC, and dries on skin in gummy strands that can be washed off with soap and water. It appears

My Favorite Finish

This concoction was handed down to me by one of my former shop managers, a concoction he called "fish oil": a mixture of 20 percent paint thinner, 40 percent oil-based polyurethane, and 40 percent linseed oil. While not the most non-toxic blend, it combines the best qualities of the component finishes — penetrative and nourishing, while drying to a hard, durable outer surface. Two coats of that, applied and buffed off, with a top-coat of wax, is a solid finish that will last for years.

milky in the can but dries clear, to a hard, plastic-like sheen (to make the surface appear more matte, apply a coat of furniture wax after the finish has cured). Since water-based is perfectly clear, it makes for a good tintable base: thoroughly mix in 5 percent of latex paint to make a translucent wash that adds color without obscuring the grain. I use water-based almost exclusively because of the easy cleanup and the lack of yellowing.

Wax is a good topcoat in any application, except on food-safe surfaces. *Paste wax* contains naphtha as a drier, which makes it toxic and bad for your skin. *Carnauba wax*, available online or at specialty stores, is pressed from palm leaves and is nontoxic as long as it is mixed with citrus driers instead of petroleum-based thinners. Much like waxing a car, wipe the finish onto a clean, dry surface, let dry for a few minutes, and then buff off. Apply wax over a poly or oil finish, or use it on wood directly. If applied to raw wood, keep in mind that it will be very difficult to get off in the future if you decide to refinish the piece. Wax protects and brings out the shine in things, and is very good for covering up scratches and small defects.

UN-TRASHCAN

Garbage bags have always struck me as one of the greatest scams in modern life. By design, they're a product that exists only to be thrown away! Trashcans are nearly as bad, just another layer of container accumulating garbage juice and bits of food in the bottom.

The Un-TrashCan is radically simple: just a frame to hold empty bags. When one is filled up, it is pulled up and out, exposing a fresh bag. All the pieces are short enough to find in dumpsters for free. Finish the assembly with several heavy coats of polyurethane to make the surface easy to clean.

MATERIALS

- Two pieces pine, 1½" × 1½" × 10"
- Two 24" 2×6s or 2×10s
- Four dowel pieces, ¾" diameter × 3"
- Wood glue
- One 18" 2×8
- Eight 3" drywall screws
- One short piece ⅜" dowel (optional; see step 5)
- Polyurethane or other finish of your choice

TOOLS

- Circular saw or table saw
- Pencil
- Tape measure
- Speed Square
- Drill/driver and ¾" drill bit
- Miter saw
- Sander

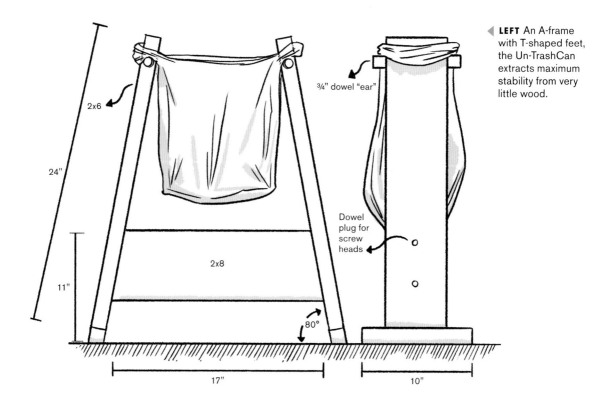

2x6

24"

11"

2x8

80°

17"

¾" dowel "ear"

Dowel plug for screw heads

10"

STEPS

1 **Using a table saw or a circular saw,** bevel one side of each of the 1½" pine strips at 10 degrees.

2 **Mark the center** (end to end) on each 10" pine strip, then mark the center (side to side) at one end of each 2×6. Glue and screw the beveled strips to the bottom of each 2×6 upright so the beveled edge faces away from the 2×6, creating two T-shaped assemblies. Countersink the screws to prevent scratching your floors.

At the opposite end of each "T", measure 1½" down and ¾" over on each side edge of the 2×6. Drill a ¾" hole, 1½" deep, and glue in a 3" section of dowel. Repeat three more times so that each "T" has dowel "ears" for hooking on the grocery bag's handles.

3 **Cut the 2×8** with opposing 10-degree miters so the long edge of the piece measures 17".

4 **Mark a centerline** down the inside and outside of each upright, parallel to the board's length. Align the mitered 2×8 on the interior centerlines, about 11" up from the bottom, and glue and screw into place. This links the uprights, forming a balanced, sturdy A-frame. Countersink the screws and plug the screw heads with a bit of ⅜" dowel, if desired.

5 **Sand the assembly** thoroughly and finish with polyurethane. Build up several coats so the surface can be wiped clean of food spills and splatters.

6 **Layer a half-dozen grocery bags** inside one another, then loop the handles over the "ears" on the top of the uprights to form a trash can.

DISPOSAL *If the screw holes are unplugged, remove the screws and break down the assembly. Strip the finish and burn or compost the wood.*

GUERILLA ROOF RACK

Foraging for material is hard work, and a little mechanical advantage can go a long way. In Chicago, scrappers prowl the alleys in overloaded pickups, harvesting metal and electronics for the recycling mills. However, you don't have to own a truck to go scavenging — a guerilla roof rack can turn any small car into a hauling machine.

The Guerilla Roof Rack is mounted with two ratchet straps and is able to handle 10-foot dimensional lumber, a half-sheet of plywood, or a big bundle of scraps. You can remove the rack frame in a few minutes, unbolt the pieces, and stow them in the trunk. I dressed up this prototype with some polyurethane and left it on the roof all winter.

MATERIALS

- Four pieces ¾" plywood, 5" × 36"
- Two 36" 2×4s
- Wood glue
- 1½" #8 galvanized or stainless-steel deck screws
- Two 36" 2×2s
- Two ¾"-wide × 16-foot-long nylon ratchet straps
- Four ½" × 4" hex-head bolts
- Four ½" hex nuts
- Eight ½" washers
- Polyurethane glue
- Two 3" × 36" rubber or non-slip foam strips (see step 6)
- Oil and exterior polyurethane finishing materials (see step 7)

TOOLS

- Pencil
- Tape
- Small plywood scrap
- Tape measure
- Jigsaw or band saw
- Sandpaper
- Staple gun
- Hammer
- Drill/driver and ⅛", ⅝", and 1¼" bits

DRAWING THE ARC

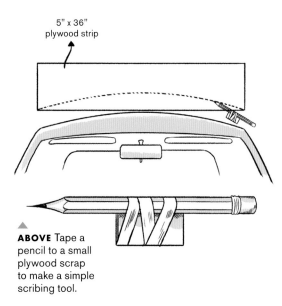

5" x 36" plywood strip

▲ **ABOVE** Tape a pencil to a small plywood scrap to make a simple scribing tool.

CUT LIST

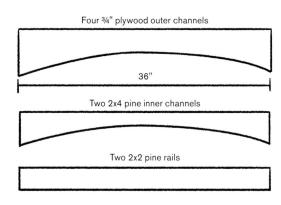

Four ¾" plywood outer channels

36"

Two 2x4 pine inner channels

Two 2x2 pine rails

INSTALLATION DIAGRAMS

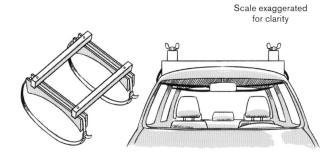

Scale exaggerated for clarity

STEPS

1 **Tape the pencil** to a small block of scrap ¾" plywood. Hold one of the plywood strips, on edge, across the roof of your car. Use a tape measure to roughly center it side to side, keeping it parallel to the windshield. Scribe the curve of the roof, running the plywood block along the roof so the pencil point traces onto the plywood, as shown at left.

2 **Cut the scribed curve** with a jigsaw or band saw. Smooth it out with sandpaper and check it for fit against the car roof, adjusting if necessary. Using the strip as a template, trace the curve onto the two 2×4s and remaining pieces of plywood, then cut and sand those pieces.

3 **Glue and screw two pieces** of plywood to the sides of each 2×4, sandwiching the 2×4 in the middle to create the crossbars. The curves should all be flush on the bottom, but on the top, the plywood should project above the 2×4, forming a channel for the nylon strap.

4 **Drill a ⅛" hole** down through the crossbars' 2×4s, 3" in from each end. On the curved underside of each crossbar, use the ⅛" hole as a centerpoint and counterbore a 1¼" hole, ¾" deep, so the bolt head will not scratch the car roof. Drill the rest of the way through each hole with a ⅝" bit; this allows some adjustment room for the bolt.

5 **Drill a ⅝" hole** 3" in from each end of each 2×2. Lay the nylon strips in the channels of the crossbars. Set the 2×2s across the crossbars as shown at left, and bolt the frame together in the corners, using the bolts, washers, and nuts.

6 **Use polyurethane glue and staples** to secure some thin rubber strips — weatherstripping, scraps of bike inner tube, or cut-up yoga mat — to the underside of the rack. This will prevent it from slipping or marring the car roof.

7 **Disassemble the rack** by removing the corner bolts. Coat the wood parts thoroughly with finish, starting with some base coats of

hand-rubbed oil, followed with a light sanding with 220-grit paper and then topped with some UV-resistant exterior ("spar") polyurethane to resist the weather.

8 **Reassemble the rack** and set it atop the car roof. Feed the nylon straps through the cabin of the car. Ratchet down tightly, but not so tight that it dents the roof. Use an additional set of straps to secure material to the rack, taking care to load it symmetrically.

DISPOSAL *Disassemble the rack, salvaging the nylon and bolts if possible. Cut the wood into small pieces so they take up less space in the trash.*

FLAT-PACK SAWHORSES

Sawhorses evolved from *sawbucks,* X-shaped assemblies of cut saplings that cradled logs for easy sawing. Eventually, the bucks developed into horses, four-legged A-frames that made great portable workbenches. They are one of the godfathers of guerilla furniture — nomadic, modular, and adaptable to dozens of uses.

These Flat-Pack Sawhorses are hinged at the leg and break down in minutes. A nylon strap tensions the legs when set up and binds the parts together when broken down. Use them on a jobsite, or as the basis for your own portable guerilla shop. With a coat of finish and some attention to craft, they are handsome enough to serve as legs for a modern dining table.

MATERIALS PER HORSE

- Four 36" 2×6s
- Four dowel pieces, ¾" diameter × 1⅝"
- Wood glue
- One 24" 2×4
- Three 1½" drywall screws
- One piece ⅝" plywood, 6" × 28"
- Two 4" door hinges
- Finishing materials of choice
- One nylon strap with tension buckle or ratchet, approximately 8 feet long

TOOLS

- Pencil
- Tape measure
- Square
- Circular saw
- Hand plane
- Drill/driver and ¾" bit
- Sandpaper
- Sander

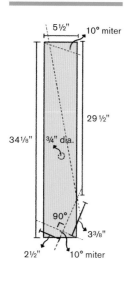

LEG CUTTING TEMPLATE

5½" 10° miter
34⅛" ¾" dia. 29½"
90°
3⅜"
2½" 10° miter

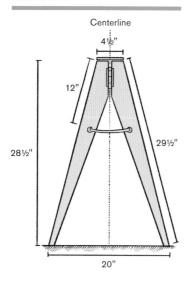

END VIEW

Centerline
4½"
12"
28½" 29½"
20"

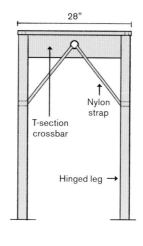

SIDE VIEW

28"
Nylon strap
T-section crossbar
Hinged leg →

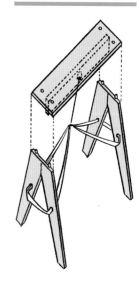

ASSEMBLY

STEPS

1 **Lay out and cut** the four 2×6 leg blanks to 34⅛" as shown above, both ends mitered, in parallel at 10 degrees.

2 **At the top end of each leg,** use a hand plane or coarse sandpaper to heavily round over the 3⅜" edges; this allows the hinges to operate freely.

3 **Drill a ¾"-diameter hole,** 1" deep, centered in the top end-grain of each leg. Make sure these holes are as straight as possible. Tap a dowel into each hole with some glue. These pegs will retain the crossbar.

4 **Drill a ¾" hole** 12" down from the top of each leg, centered on the width of the leg. Round off the edges with a scrap of sandpaper rolled into a little tube. This will keep the sharp edges of the hole from wearing away at the nylon strap.

5 **Glue and screw the 2×4 piece** to the plywood strip, centered end-to-end and left-to-right, forming a T-section. The 2×4 should fall short of the ends of the plywood by 2" at each end. Drill a ¾" hole in the center of the 2×4, then sand the edges.

6 **Finish the wood parts** with product of your choice. I used mineral oil and wax on this pair.

7 **Join each pair of legs** with a hinge at the top, laying the plates of the hinges flat on the broad surface of each leg. Use a square to make sure that the legs align across the top and fold evenly together.

8 **Lay the T-section crossbar** upside down on the floor so the plywood plate is flat against the floor. Set the legs, unfolded, on each end and trace the location of the dowel plugs onto the plywood. Drill the four ¾" holes through the plywood.

9 **To set up the horses,** drop the legs onto the cross-bar so that the four dowels go into the four holes in the plywood plate. Lace the nylon strap through the hole in the crossbar, down through one set of legs, back through the center hole, down through the other set of legs, and back to the center, as shown in the photos. Tighten until the horse is sturdy. Flip over.

DISPOSAL *Disassemble, salvaging the hinges and strap for future use. Compost or burn the legs. Throw out the crossbar.*

DOOR DESK

Every door dreams of retiring as a desk (or a table). After spending years defending against weather, intruders, and relentless knocking, a door deserves to lie down on a sturdy base and rest. This flat-packable workstation has survived three moves so far, and served as the platform for writing most of this book.

The Door Desk mates a beautiful, timeworn door with a demountable trestle base. Pieces of plate aluminum (old road signs) are cut and inlaid to flush out the panels. Depending on available material, the door panels could also be filled with concrete, grout, wood scraps, or glass.

MATERIALS
- Four 28" 2×4s
- Two 24" 2×4s
- Wood glue
- 3" drywall screws
- Old solid-wood panel door, preferably with panels of equal size
- One 2×4, approximately 72" long (for a standard 80" door)
- 1½" drywall screws
- Plate aluminum or other filler material (size and quantity as needed)
- Construction adhesive
- Six ¼" × 4" lag bolts with washers
- One 75" 2×2 or other material (see step 9)

TOOLS
- Clamps
- Pencil
- Tape measure
- Square
- Circular saw
- Hammer
- Chisel
- Miter saw
- Straightedge
- Drill/driver and 1", ¾", and ¼" bits

STEPS

1 **Clamp the four** 28" 2×4s together, on edge, making sure the ends are precisely aligned; these will become the legs. Using the square, mark a line over all four pieces, 3½" from the ends. Set the circular saw blade to a depth of 2" and a bevel of 5 degrees, and run a series of closely spaced parallel cuts over all four boards, from your mark out toward the end of the boards, as shown below. Knock out the waste with a hammer and chisel. Each leg should now have an L-shaped notch in one end that is 2" × 3½", canted at a 5-degree angle.

2 **Miter both ends** of each leg, in parallel, at 5 degrees.

3 **Measure 1½" over** from the edge opposite the notch at the bottom (non-notched) end of each leg. Use a long straightedge to draw a line connecting that mark with the bottom outside corner of the notch. Cut the taper on each leg.

4 **Complete the leg assemblies** by securing the 24" crosspieces in the leg notches with some wood glue and 3" drywall screws driven

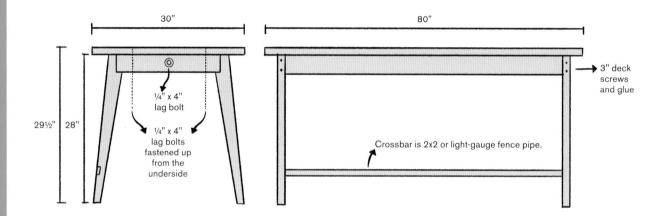

TIP Remove the six lag bolts, pop out the crossbar, and the desk breaks down. All the pieces will fit in a minivan, small pickup, or on a guerilla roof rack.

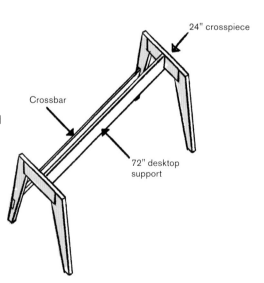

NOTCHING THE LEGS

Clamp the four leg blanks together and run a circular saw over them. Chisel out the waste.

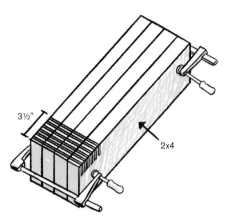

through the outside edges of the legs. Lay out the screws neatly, staggering and predrilling the screw holes to prevent splitting. Counterbore a 1"-diameter × ¾"-deep hole in the center of each crosspiece. Then drill a ¼" hole all the way through at the center of the counterbore.

5   **Find the center of the door,** end to end, then make a centerline across the door's width on what will be the underside of the desktop. For a standard door, this should be about 40" in from each end. Mark a centerline on the 72" 2×4, and align this with the centerline on the door. Scribe the panel locations in the door onto the 2×4. Notch the 2×4 so that it will lie flush to the underside of the door, with the notches fitting over the rails (horizontal door frame parts). Use the same method as when notching the legs, creating a series of parallel cuts with a circular saw, then knocking out the waste with a chisel.

6   **Glue and screw the 72" support** to the underside of the door, using 1½" screws, as shown at right. Screw through the top face of the door — through the panels — so the screw heads will be hidden later by the aluminum plates.

7   **Fill in the recessed panels** on the top side of the door with aluminum, plywood, hardboard, glass, concrete, or plastic pieces that flush out the surface, making a smooth, continuous top. I used aluminum road signs, turned upside down and adhered with construction adhesive.

8   **Center the leg frames** on each end and use one lag bolt at each end to attach the 72" desktop support to the 24" crosspieces. Use two more lag bolts per leg frame to go up into the underside of the desk; the counterbore pilot holes ensure the bolt heads are recessed into the crosspieces.

9   **Install a support bar,** or stretcher, low on the back legs to provide more lateral stiffness. This piece runs parallel to the length of the desktop. It could be a 2×2, a piece of pipe or scrap wood, or an X-shaped wire brace. For this version,

I used a salvaged chain-link fence top bar, secured by friction-fit in a hole in each back leg and pinned with a drywall screw.

DISPOSAL *Disassemble the frame into constituent parts, recycling the legs and fasteners for another piece of furniture. Cut the door up for the landfill or compost pile.*

TABLETOP AND SUPPORT

The support under the door gives the frame lateral stability.

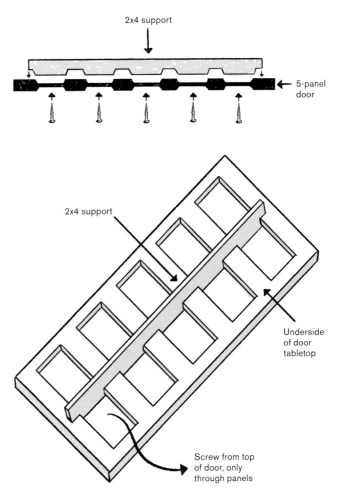

2x4 support

5-panel door

2x4 support

Underside of door tabletop

Screw from top of door, only through panels

BREAK-DOWN TABLE

Every kitchen, no matter how small, needs a cheerful little corner for having a cup of coffee in the morning. The usual solution is a rickety card table, papered with some plastic imitation of wood and stained with a thousand mug rings.

The Break-Down Table brings some dignity to those dark early mornings before work. A warm wooden sheet sits on four legs that tenon through the tabletop, ornamenting the surface with a glimpse of the structure. Each leg unscrews and pops out, breaking the table down into five light pieces.

MATERIALS

- Two pieces ⅝" plywood, 32" to 40" square
- Wood glue
- 1" drywall screws
- Four 38" 2×4s
- Four ¾"-diameter × 10" hardwood dowels
- Paint or other finish of your choice
- Eight 2" drywall screws
- Eight #10 washers

TOOLS

- Pencil
- Tape measure
- Circular saw and straightedge guide
- Router (optional)
- Drill/driver and ⅜" and ¾" bits
- Jigsaw
- Chisel
- Mallet
- Miter saw
- Speed Square
- Orbital sander

MORTISE AND SCREW LAYOUT

Space drywall screws on a 6" grid, countersinking for a smooth surface.

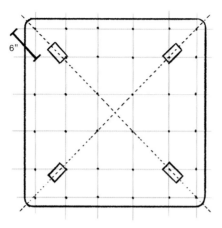

MORTISE DETAIL

Cut mortises with a jigsaw, staying slightly inside the lines for a tight fit.

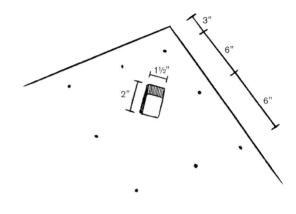

STEPS

1 **Breakfast tables** are typically 32" to 40" to a side; customize the dimensions to fit your available space. This example is 34" square. Cut the plywood with a circular saw and a straightedge to about 4" larger than your desired finished dimensions, producing two pieces of equal size. For example, for a 34" square table, cut the pieces at 38" × 38".

2 **Laminate the two pieces together** with glue and 1" screws. Spread a thin, even layer of common wood glue over the mating surfaces, and then countersink and screw together from one side only. Space the screws in a 6" grid, with a rim of screws about 3" in from the edges all around, as shown above left. Let the glue cure for at least 8 hours.

3 **Cut the tabletop down** to its finished size, using a clamped straightedge with the circular saw to slice 2" off each side. This trimming ensures everything is flush and tight and the edges appear perfect. Sand the top and ease the edges to prevent splinters. If you prefer, round over or chamfer the edges with a router.

4 **Using a straightedge and pencil,** connect the diagonally opposing corners of the tabletop with lines to form an X. Measure in 6" from each corner, then lay out a 1½" × 2" box, starting at the 6" line and moving toward the center of the table. Each box should be centered on and aligned with its X line, with the 2" dimension parallel to the line and the 1½" dimension perpendicular to the line, as shown above right.

5 **Drill a ⅜" hole** in each corner of each box, slightly inside the lines. Rough-cut the mortises with a jigsaw, then refine with a chisel, as shown above right. Plywood does not chisel easily, so you may have to carve carefully with the jigsaw. Make sure these holes are as accurate as possible, as the stability of the table depends on a tight fit.

6 **Using a pencil and a straightedge,** connect the opposite corners of each 2×4. Cut the tapers with a circular saw.

7 **Cut the legs to length** on the miter saw, making sure to register the factory edge of each 2×4 piece against the fence for each cut. Miter the fat end of each piece to 7 degrees, cutting away as little length as possible. Miter the skinny end of each piece, parallel to the top miter, at 31¾".

8 **Lay out the tenons** on the fat end of each leg, marking a rectangle that's 1¼" tall × 2" wide, centered in the width of the 2×4, as shown

below. The most important aspect of laying out the tenons is that the horizontals of the two notches are parallel to the top and bottom of the leg (at the same 7-degree angle). The vertical parts of the notches must be perpendicular to the horizontals. All this geometry will ensure that the legs are angled but the tabletop is level. Measure down 1¼" from the top of the leg and draw a horizontal line that's parallel to the leg's end. Find the center of that line, then measure 1" to either side and mark a vertical line that's perpendicular to the horizontal line.

9 **Cut out the notches** with a jigsaw to create the tenons, being careful to stay a little outside of the lines. Test-fit each leg in each mortise, paring away at the tenon with a chisel until it fits tightly and the tenon shoulders seat firmly against the underside of the table.

10 **Drill a ¾" hole** that is tangent to the bottom of the shoulders of the tenon and centered on the width of the tenon. Tap a 10" length of dowel

into the hole with a little glue, centering it so 4¼" projects on either side, as shown below. This bar provides lateral stability.

11 **Lightly sand all parts** and finish as desired. To assemble, lay the tabletop flat on the floor, bottom facing up. Insert a leg into each mortise, making sure the shoulders of the tenon seat firmly against the underside of the tabletop and the leg is angled toward the perimeter of the table. Predrill and screw through each dowel "ear" and into the underside of the tabletop with a 2" drywall screw and a #10 washer. Flip the table over.

DISPOSAL *This table breaks down into five easy pieces: the plywood must be thrown out, but, depending on your choice of finish, the legs could be recycled into other projects, burned as kindling, or composted.*

LEG CUTTING TEMPLATE

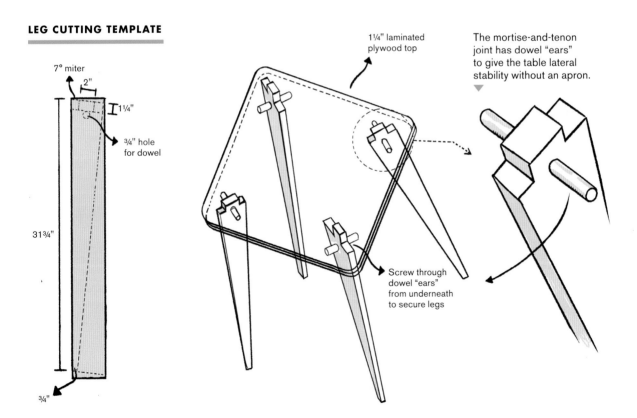

7° miter

2"

1¼"

¾" hole for dowel

31¾"

¾"

1¼" laminated plywood top

The mortise-and-tenon joint has dowel "ears" to give the table lateral stability without an apron.

Screw through dowel "ears" from underneath to secure legs

FLAT-PACK SHELVES

Shelves seem to be sturdy, cheap, or good-looking, but never all three at once. The big-box models are flimsy, racking diagonally after a few months. Handsome shelving systems cost way too much, and the really sturdy ones look like they escaped from some stock-room purgatory. The guerilla might give up, leaving books boxed, closeted, or milk-crated. But they deserve better!

The Flat-Pack Shelves are plywood with a pop of color on the cut edges. The tapered form attenuates to the top, grading books by size and weight for maximum stability. Sturdy box-framed shelves are bolted to the uprights to create a solid, rack-free structure. When it comes time to move, the unit breaks down into five pieces in 15 minutes.

MATERIALS

- One 4×8-foot sheet ¾" plywood
- 1½" #6 screws, Spax or other fine-thread type preferred
- ⅜" dowel (for optional plugs)
- Wood glue
- Finish of your choice
- Twelve ½" × 2" coarse-thread galvanized hex-head bolts
- Twelve ½" nuts
- Twenty-four ½" cut washers

TOOLS

- Pencil
- Tape measure
- Circular saw and straight-edge guide
- Straightedge
- Square
- Drill/driver and 1¼" and ⅝" bits
- Table saw (optional)
- Miter saw (optional)
- Clamps
- Orbital sander
- Sanding block, 100-grit
- Ratchet wrench
- Crescent wrench

4×8 PLYWOOD CUT DIAGRAM

All of the parts come out of a standard sheet of plywood, making this design easy to adapt to CNC routing.

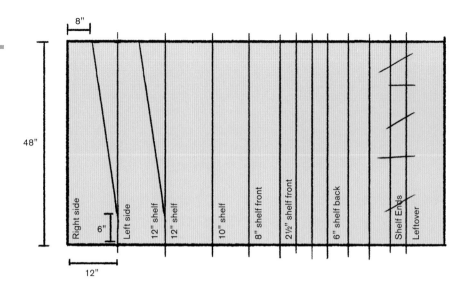

8"

48"

Right side | 6" | Left side | 12" shelf | 12" shelf | 10" shelf | 8" shelf front | 2½" shelf front | 6" shelf back | Shelf Ends | Leftover

12"

SHELF LAYOUT FOR ASSEMBLY

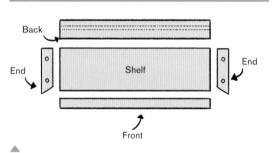

Back

End ← ← End

Shelf

Front

ABOVE Each shelf is an open-bottom box, which stiffens the surface and provides lateral stability without a back.

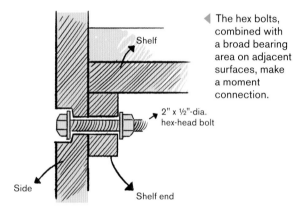

Shelf

◀ The hex bolts, combined with a broad bearing area on adjacent surfaces, make a moment connection.

2" × ½"-dia. hex-head bolt

Side

Shelf end

ELEVATIONS

The slight taper of the sides, combined with varied shelf spacing, accommodates a wide variety of media. It also serves as a sturdy stepladder in a pinch.

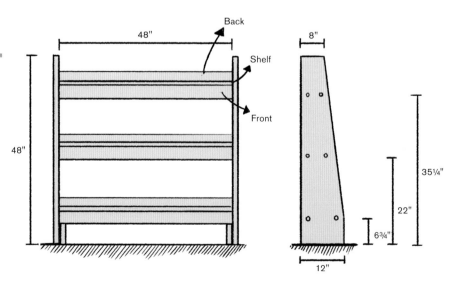

Back

48"

Shelf

Front

48"

8"

35¼"

22"

6¾"

12"

STEPS

1 **Cut two plywood blanks** for the sides, 12" wide × 48" long. Use a clamped straightedge guide and a finishing blade to ensure a clean cut. Measure 6" up one long edge of each piece and make a mark. At the opposite end, measure 8" over along the short side. Connect the two marks and cut the taper, which works out to be about 5 degrees off vertical. This will be the front edge of the sides of the shelves.

2 **Measuring up from the bottom** of each side piece, make a mark at 6¾", 22", and 35¼". Use a square, registered on the back edge of the side piece, to draw a straight horizontal line at each mark. Drill two holes on each line, centered 2¼" in from each side edge, as shown at left. Start with a 1¼" counterbore that only goes ⅜" deep into the plywood, followed by a ⅝" hole that goes all the way through. The extra ⅛" tolerance in the bolt hole will compensate for any construction inaccuracies when assembling the piece.

3 **Cut one shelf each** at 8" × 48", 10" × 48", and 12" × 48". Cut three plywood shelf backs at 6" × 48".

4 **Cut three plywood shelf fronts** at 2½" × 48", with each long edge beveled in parallel at 5 degrees, to match the taper of the side pieces. A table saw is helpful here for maximum accuracy, but you can also set the blade of a circular saw at a bevel, clamp down a straightedge, and make your cuts.

5 **Cut two strips of plywood** at 2½" × 48". From the strips, cut six shelf end pieces — with one end square-cut (90 degrees) and the other end mitered at 5 degrees. Measuring to the short side of the miter, cut two end pieces to length at 7½", two at 8¾", and two at 10⅛". Drill two ⅝" holes, 1½" in from each end and centered vertically, matching the holes on the shelf sides.

6 **Cut two pieces,** 6" wide × 12" long, out of whatever plywood material remains. Glue and screw them to the inside of the side pieces, directly below the bottom shelf. Make sure that the sides are mirror images of each other. This doubles the thickness of the feet for better stability.

7 **Sand all pieces,** but be careful not to go through the veneer of the plywood. Ease the edges with a sanding block.

8 **Apply the finish** of your choice. If desired, tape off all the exposed end-grain edges and paint with a bright enamel. This outlines the form and hides the cut edges, but it is time-consuming.

9 **Assemble the unit** by laying all the shelves on the floor, on their backs. Lay the sides, front edges up, to the outsides of the shelves, and bolt through each hole with a washer on each side. Use a wrench to hold the bolt on the inside while tightening with the ratchet on the outside.

DISPOSAL *These shelves should last a very long time. The structure is incredibly strong, and their flat-pack nature makes them easy to move. If you must get rid of them, donate to a thrift store.*

BEDSIDE TABLE

For years, I had a stack of milk crates as a bedside table. Many guerillas have gone down this route in moments of weakness and desperation. But, there are drawbacks: little surface area for pocket ephemera; the molded pattern collects dust; and the general aesthetic is more slacker-chic than grown-up adult.

The Bedside Table is a versatile piece, whether as a nightstand, temporary desk, or end table. Two asymmetrical A-frames are bolted to a box that both braces the legs and provides surface and storage. The suspended box, in this case plywood, could also be a readymade — an old drawer, a salvaged cabinet, or an antique wooden crate.

MATERIALS

- Two pieces $5/8$" plywood, 18" × 22"
- Two pieces $5/8$" plywood, 8" × 18"
- One piece $5/8$" plywood, 8" × 20¾"
- Wood glue
- 2½" galvanized coarse-thread #8 deck screws
- Finish of your choice
- Four 32" 2×4s
- One 12" 2×4
- Two ¾"-diameter × 18" dowels
- Eight ½" × 2½" hex-head bolts
- Eight ½" cut washers

TOOLS

- Pencil
- Tape measure
- Straightedge
- Circular saw
- Square
- Ratchet wrench
- Wrench
- Miter saw
- Drill/driver and ¼", $5/8$", ¾", 1" bits
- Orbital sander with 100- and 120-grit sandpaper

STEPS

1 Cut the five plywood pieces to these dimensions: 2 at 18" × 22", 2 at 8" × 18", and 1 at 8" × 20¾". If desired, run a dado in one of the large panels, about ⅝" wide × ⅜" deep, to accommodate propping a smartphone on edge (see previous page). If using a ready-made box, skip to step 4.

2 On each 8" × 18" side piece, measure 2½" in from each side at three of the four corners and drill a ⅝" hole. For the fourth bolt hole, measure 3½" along the long side and 2½" down.

3 Sand the plywood pieces. Assemble the plywood box with glue and screws. The top and bottom should capture the sides, and the back should be captured by the sides, top, and bottom. Make sure the sides are mirror images

of one another, so that the angled pair of bolt holes and the vertical pair of bolt holes align with one another. Finish the box as desired.

4 On each 2×4, make a mark 1¼" in from one long edge, then connect that mark with a diagonal line to the opposite corner of the board. Use a circular saw to split the pieces along that line, producing four tapered legs.

5 Rip a 12" length of 2×4 in half lengthwise with the circular saw (or a table saw, if available), producing two pieces about 1¾" wide. Cut these to length at 9¾" to create the two crossbars, mitering one end at 5°.

6 At the fat end of two of the legs, lay out a 1" × 1¾" notch (see next page). While the notch should be cut out of the tapered side of the leg, it should be square to the factory edge of the leg. Use the miter saw to cut these back legs to 29½", removing material only from the bottom (non-notched) end.

7 Miter the two front legs at 5 degrees, in parallel, making sure to register the factory edge of the leg against the fence of the miter saw. Cut them to 30" long. At the fat end of each leg, lay out a notch that is 1" × 1¾". Again, the notch should be cut out of the tapered side of the leg, but this time it should be square to the top of the leg. The vertical portion of the notch should be parallel to the factory edge of the leg, and the horizontal portion of the notch should be parallel to the top (mitered) end of the leg.

8 Make a mark 6" up from the bottom of each leg, on the tapered side. Drill a ¾" hole halfway into the depth of the material. The best way to do this is to lay the factory edge of the leg on a level surface, tapered surface facing up, and concentrate on keeping the drill bit perfectly plumb as you make the hole.

9 Assemble the legs by gluing and screwing the crossbar into the leg notches. Install a 14¾" length of dowel into the holes near the bottom of the legs, securing with glue and a single screw driven through the leg and into each dowel end (predrill first).

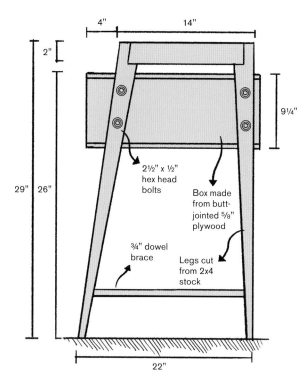

4"   14"

2"

9¼"

29"   26"

2½" x ½" hex head bolts

Box made from butt-jointed ⅝" plywood

¾" dowel brace

Legs cut from 2x4 stock

22"

SIDE VIEW The simple bolt connections allow this piece to knock flat in minutes. I used salvaged old-growth 2×4s, which had white tiger-striping on the narrow edges from plaster and lath.

10 Scribe the holes in the boxes onto the legs, positioning the leg assembly so it extends 3" above the top surface of the box. The straight leg should be toward the back of the box, and the slanted leg toward the front. The back edge of the back legs should be 1¼" in from the back edge of the box. On the outside face of the legs, use each ¼" hole to center a 1" counterbore that goes about ¾" into the wood. Complete the hole with a ⅝" bit.

11 Assemble by matching the holes in the box to those on the legs and bolting through with ½" by 2½" hex-head bolts and washers.

DISPOSAL *This piece disassembles into three pieces, making it easy to pack flat and move, ship, or give away. If necessary, recycle the hardware, throw out the box, and compost the legs.*

BOX ASSEMBLY

A simple butt-jointed box, glued and screwed, can be made out of any sort of sheet material. Replace with a readymade if available.

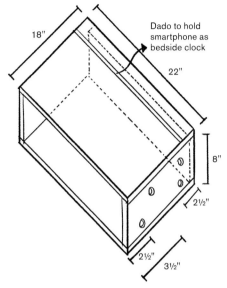

NOTCHING THE BACK LEGS

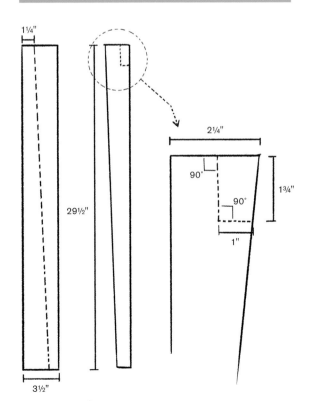

NOTCHING THE FRONT LEGS

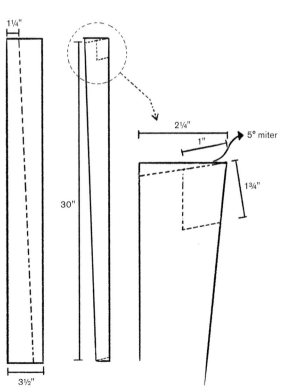

SCRAP LAMP

Wire spools are an old readymade — plywood circles with bolt-on legs, stained and put on the patio. One decorated our garage for years and got hauled out for cookouts every Fourth of July. It was rickety, splintery, and rough; just right for the dog days of summer. The Scrap Lamp rescues two plywood discs from a spool of wire and strings them together with strips of scrap wood, creating a striated drum. An aluminum studio lamp is mounted in the top disc, casting light down and through the slats, creating a warm, woody glow.

MATERIALS

- Plywood wire spool, 10" to 12" in diameter or two pieces ¾" plywood, approximately 12" square
- Scrap wood strips (see step 5)
- Wood glue
- Brads
- Two or three 16d nails
- One 6" aluminum studio lamp
- Velcro tape

TOOLS

- Wrench
- Pencil
- Tape measure
- Compass or round objects for tracing
- Drill/driver and ⅜" bit
- Jigsaw
- Square
- Miter saw
- Brad nailer
- Scissors

STEPS

1 **Disassemble the wire spool,** salvaging the two circular ends. Lacking a spool, cut two 12"-diameter discs out of plywood with the jigsaw. The exact diameter is unimportant; just trace anything circular that's handy and in the neighborhood of 12".

2 **Center a 5"-diameter object** (or a compass) onto one of the plywood discs and trace around it to mark a circle. Drill a ⅜" hole inside the circle, insert the jigsaw blade, and cut out the circle, creating a ring. This is the top of the lamp.

3 **Repeat the same process** on the second disc, using an 8" object (or a compass) to create an 8" hole. This is the bottom of the lamp.

4 **Holding the top and bottom rings together,** use the square to mark three or four reference marks across the edges of both pieces, perpendicular to the flat faces of the rings. These will help you keep the structure aligned as you add the strips.

5 **Cut 24 strips of wood** to random lengths. The strips can be anything – plaster lath, offcuts, pallet wood, pieces of molding, door trim, etc. At least three of the longest strips should be the same length (approximately 60"); these will become the legs, and must stand evenly on the floor.

6 **Lay out the strips** on your work surface so the sides that will be on the outside of the completed lamp are facing down. Measuring from the same end on each strip, make a mark at 6" and 24". Use the square to draw a horizontal line across the strip at each mark; these indicate where the strips align with the plywood rings.

7 **Add a dab of glue** to a strip just below the 6" mark, and attach the top ring, aligning it with the mark. Nail through the strip and into the ring with a brad. Do the same with the second ring, at the 24" mark. It is best to do this with the strip and the rings set on edge on a worktable so that the

PLYWOOD DISCS OR ENDS OF WIRE SPOOLS

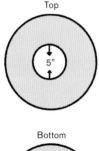

Top

5"

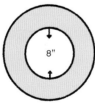

Bottom

8"

LAYOUT OF RANDOM LENGTHS OF SCRAP WOOD STRIPS

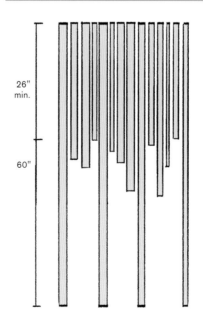

26" min.

60"

CROSS-SECTION OF ASSEMBLED LAMP

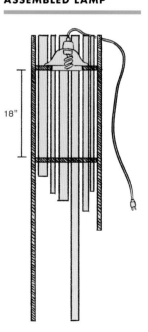

18"

rings are just tangent to the flat face of the strip. To keep them from rolling away, put a clamp on each ring, which will stabilize it side-to-side in the upright position. If you don't have access to a brad nailer, use (carefully) hand-driven finish nails or #6 wood screws. Be sure to predrill, as both the rings and strips will be vulnerable to splitting.

8 **The assembly will be very wobbly** at first but will stiffen with each additional strip. Check that the first strip is square to the rings by registering the square against the rings. Using two or three 16d nails as spacers, position a second strip of different length against the first, gluing and nailing into place.

9 **Continue installing strips** all the way around the rings, alternating length with each strip.

Space the 60" leg strips equidistantly around the circumference of the rings to form a stable tripod when the lamp is stood up.

10 **Apply three pieces of Velcro tape** to the edge of the studio lampshade, and three matching pieces around the edge of the 5"-diameter hole in the top ring. Stand the structure up and stick the lamp in place (see step 4 of the Cube Lamp on page 33).

DISPOSAL *Pull off and reuse, donate, or recycle the studio lamp. Remove the strips and compost, burn, or recycle. Throw away the plywood rings.*

TWO-TONE TABLE

MATERIALS

- One 2×6-foot piece of cardboard
- Four to six 8-foot 2×8s
- One 8-foot cedar 2×4 (or other contrasting wood)
- Seven ½"-diameter × 36" threaded rods
- Fourteen ½" nuts and washers
- Wood glue
- 2 pounds 2½" drywall screws
- Four 22"-long pieces of 1"-thick lumber
- Two 49"-long pieces of 1"-thick lumber
- One ½" diameter × 24" pine dowel
- Finish of your choice

TOOLS

- Pencil
- Tape measure
- Square
- Protractor
- Ruler or straightedge
- Table saw
- Craft knife or box cutter
- Miter saw
- Hammer or mallet
- Drill/driver and ⅝" and 1" spade bits
- Clamps
- Ratchet straps (optional)
- Ratchet wrench
- Rotary tool or hacksaw
- Belt sander with 80-, 100-, and 120-grit sanding belts
- Orbital sander with 120-grit sandpaper

In an age of digital proliferation, coffee tables suffer from clutter like never before. There are the remotes, the phones, the laptops, the tablets, and then, of course, the old-fashioned magazines and cans of beer. The Two-Tone Table solves this problem with a shelf under the top surface, perfect for stashing the devices so the top can be put to use for food and drinks. The majority of the components are cheap pine studs, salvaged from a jobsite, laminated together with threaded rods. A racing stripe of red cedar shoots through the middle, splitting the monolithic form and giving this table its name.

STEPS

1 **Construct a full-size template** out of a sheet of cardboard, corrugated plastic, or butcher paper, following the side views in the Face Frame diagram on the next page. The top is 48" long, the legs 19⅛", canting out at a 20-degree angle, and the structure is 1½" thick throughout. This template will help you keep track of the pieces during construction.

2 **Cut down the 2×8s** (or 2×4s, 2×6s, 2×10s . . . whatever lumber you can salvage or buy cheapest) into 1½"-square blanks on the table saw. First cut the pieces about ¼" oversize, then flip and run the opposite edge through the saw. This takes more time but helps create the straightest boards, eliminating gaps during assembly.

3 **Cut the blanks to length.** There are two sets of alternating layers of wood. One layer consists of three pieces: one top and two legs; the other consists of six pieces: one top, one shelf, two filler strips, and two legs. Use the template to mark the

lengths and miters on each piece. All of the miters are 20 degrees and vary only in orientation. Cut pieces for each of the two types of layers and test-fit them to make sure all looks good. Then, set up a stop block (see box on page 98) and cut enough strips for seven three-piece layers and six six-piece layers (see cut list below; this will yield an approximately 21½"-wide table). Arrange the pieces into two stacks, one for each type of layer.

4 **Locate the centers of all your joints** in the template and poke a hole (see diagrams at right). Use the template to transfer the hole locations to all of the pieces, then drill each hole with a ⅝" spade bit. For the six pieces that will become the two outer layers (2 **C** pieces and 4 **D** pieces), first drill a 1"-diameter × ¾"-deep counterbore, then drill the ⅝" through-hole; the counterbores will accept the nuts on the threaded rods.

5 **Starting with the counterbored outer strips,** begin to build up the table, one layer of strips at a time, using the threaded rods as registration devices. Smear each strip with a thin, even layer of wood glue and screw to the previous set of strips with drywall screws. Predrill to prevent splitting. Take care in placing your contrasting wood strip for maximum aesthetic effect. Do not glue in the shelf pieces yet; just set them in and use them for alignment. Stop at seven layers, and let the assembly dry overnight. Repeat for the remaining six layers to create a matching half.

6 **Assemble the table in two halves,** leaving the shelf pieces out. Push the threaded rods through one half, smear the wood with glue – a hybrid of yellow glue and polyurethane glue works well here – and drop the second half onto the first. Hammer them together with a mallet. Use two ratchets to crank the threaded rods to force the sides together. Apply ratchet straps or clamps if needed. Allow to dry overnight.

7 **Remove the threaded rods** from the table. Use scraps, shims, slivers, and sawdust, along with glue, to fill any cracks that refuse to close; let

SIDE VIEW

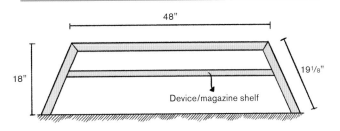

48"

18"

19⅛"

Device/magazine shelf

3-PIECE LAYER

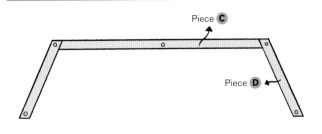

Piece **C**

Piece **D**

6-PIECE LAYER

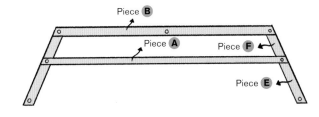

Piece **B**

Piece **A**

Piece **F**

Piece **E**

CUT LIST

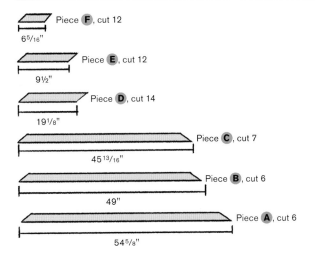

Piece **F**, cut 12

6⁵⁄₁₆"

Piece **E**, cut 12

9½"

Piece **D**, cut 14

19⅛"

Piece **C**, cut 7

45¹³⁄₁₆"

Piece **B**, cut 6

49"

Piece **A**, cut 6

54⅝"

Stop Block Setup

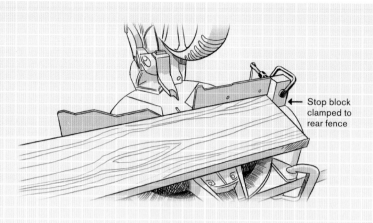

Stop block clamped to rear fence

Setting up a stop on your miter saw can save a lot of work when cutting multiple pieces at the same length. Clamp a block to the miter saw at the desired distance from the blade, then chock to the block with your material: cut, slide, chock; cut, slide, chock . . .

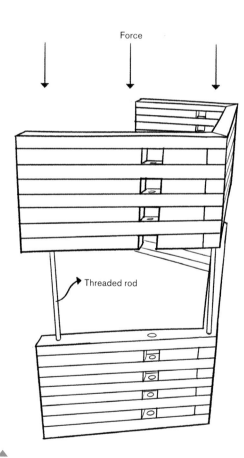

Force

Threaded rod

▲ **ASSEMBLY** Threaded rods serve as built-in clamps, forcing the two halves of the table together. Over time, they will prevent twisting and warping from seasonal expansion and contraction in the wood.

dry. Sand the whole structure, top and bottom, with a belt sander and an 80-grit belt for flushness, then follow with 100- and 120-grit belts to get to the finished surface. Sand the shelf strips separately, then insert them into the slots left during assembly. Run the threaded rods through and tighten.

8 **Cut 1"-thick mitered finish strips** to cap the side edges of the table and cover the exposed ends of the threaded rods. Trim off any excess rod flush with a hacksaw, rotary tool, or angle grinder. Install the strips with glue and screws, counterboring and plugging the screw heads with bits of dowel. Sand the dowel plugs flush and finish the table as desired.

DISPOSAL *This table is monolithic and nearly indestructible. If you no longer have a need for it, donate it to a charity or a neighbor.*

SCRAP TABLE

Nothing beats a gathering of friends around a big
table, raucous with laughter, food, and wine. Nothing
brings a room of strangers together like sitting at a
community table on bench seating, elbows rubbing.
The Scrap Table is 12 feet of gathering goodness, made
of lots of tiny pieces laminated with glue and threaded
rods. A trestle base is laminated right into the top,
making structure and surface inseparable. All the
variegated pieces, planed and sanded smooth, turn
the wood into petrified strata.

MATERIALS

- Two 8-foot 2×6s
- Two 8-foot 2×8s
- Wood glue
- 1 pound 3" coarse-thread
  #8 drywall or deck screws
- Scrap wood strips,
  1¾" to 4" wide
- 2 pounds 2½" coarse-thread
  #8 drywall or deck screws
- Five ½"-diameter × 36"
  galvanized threaded rods
- Ten ½" galvanized nuts
- Ten ½" galvanized washers
- Polyurethane glue
- Two ¾"-diameter × 36"
  galvanized threaded rods
- Eight ¾" galvanized nuts
- Sixteen ¾" galvanized
  washers
- Finish of your choice

TOOLS

- Pencil
- Tape measure
- Miter saw
- Block plane
- Drill/driver and ⅝" and
  1" spade bits
- Square
- Circular saw and straight-
  edge guide
- Ratchet wrench
- Clamps (optional)
- Ratchet straps (optional)
- Hacksaw
- Locking pliers
- Belt sander and 80- and
  100-grit belts
- Orbital sander with
  120-grit sandpaper

STEPS

1 **Cut the 2×6s** into eight 48" blanks for the legs. Mark a diagonal line from corner to corner of each leg piece, then cut each into two triangles with the circular saw. You should end up with eight leg blanks that are 5½" wide at one end and sharply pointed (0" wide) at the other.

2 **Miter the wide end** of each leg to 15 degrees, making sure to register the factory edge of each blank against the saw's fence. Cut off as little as possible to achieve the miter. Measuring from the freshly mitered end, along the factory edge, cut each leg to length at 31", with a 15-degree miter that's parallel to the first. Ease all cut edges lightly with a block plane or sanding block.

3 **Measure up 8"** from the thin (floor end) of each leg and drill a 1" hole, centered in the width of the piece.

4 **Prepare the 2×8 trestle boards** by making two marks along the bottom edge of each board, 18" in from the ends. Then make a mark 2" down from the top at the end of each board. Connect these two marks and cut with a circular saw to create the taper, as shown at right. Ease all cut edges lightly with a block plane or sanding block.

5 **Align one leg** on one trestle so that the wide end of the leg is flush with the top of the trestle and the factory edge intersects the end of the taper in the trestle, as shown at right. Glue and screw the pieces with four 3" screws. Repeat to install the seven remaining legs, creating two trestle assemblies.

6 **Lay one trestle** on the ground. Begin building up the tabletop by applying an even coat of glue to a strip of wood and fasten it onto the trestle with 2½" screws so the top of the strip is flush with the top of the trestle. Continue in this fashion, building up strips of wood with glue and screws. As you build up the strips, use a straightedge to check that the top surface is remaining flush, flat, and square to the broad face of the trestles. The intent of this design is to make a large table out of otherwise wasted small scraps, so feel free to piece together tiny bits; just make sure that each layer is made of a consistent thickness of wood, and that the seams are well-glued and lapped from layer to layer. Around the legs, miter the ends of the strips to match the angle of the 2×6s, locking the legs into the tabletop. Stop when you have built up about 3" of strips on one side of each trestle.

LEG CUTTING TEMPLATE

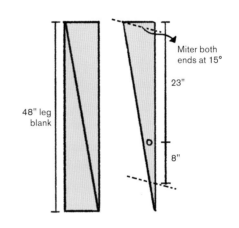

48" leg blank

Miter both ends at 15°

23"

8"

TRESTLE BASE

The 2×8 trestles are laminated into the tabletop itself, eliminating the need for an apron and making the thin top appear to "float."

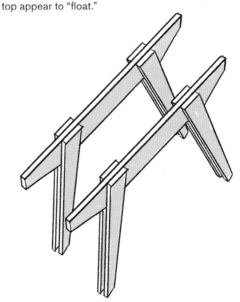

Using small pieces of wood of dissimilar species is usually a recipe for delamination. Pinning the scraps with threaded rods keeps the surface stable over time.

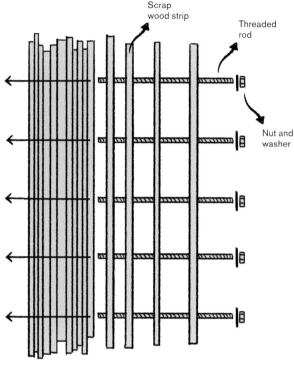

Scrap wood strip

Threaded rod

Nut and washer

7 Lay out five lines: one in the center, end-to-end; two each centered on the legs; and at about 64" from each side of the centerline (this will be about 8" in from the ends of a 12-foot table; adjust according to your planned length). Drill holes at these lines with a ⅝" spade bit, taking care to drill perfectly vertically. As you add layers to the tabletop, you will continue to drill these holes, eventually creating lines of holes for the threaded rods that penetrate through the whole tabletop, as shown at left.

8 Continue building up one side of each trestle until you have 10" to 12" of strips, then flip the assembly and build up the other side about 5", continuing to drill holes for the threaded rods. Aim for a total tabletop width of 30" to 34" (15" to 17" for each trestle assembly). Be sure to keep the total width under 36" so the threaded rods will reach all the way through.

9 Gather a group of friends to assemble the table. Push the five ½" threaded rods through the five holes in one half of the top so the rods stick out of the middle an inch or two. Coat the middle seam of both halves of the tabletop with a mixture of standard wood glue and polyurethane glue, making sure not to leave any dry spots.

SIDE VIEW The scrap table is a modified trestle design, running supports parallel to the long sides of the table. This strategy lengthens and lightens the silhouette, making a very large table appear quite delicate.

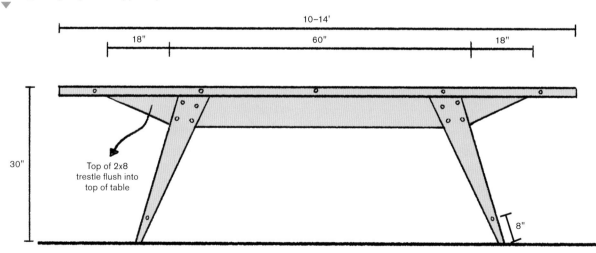

10–14'

18"   60"   18"

30"

Top of 2x8 trestle flush into top of table

8"

Stand up the second half and align it with the first half, pushing the threaded rods all the way through the structure. They may need some persuasion with a mallet. Alternately, chuck the end of the rod into a ½" drill and run it forward, effectively screwing the rod through.

10 **Once the rods are through,** sticking out both sides a little bit, put on washers and nuts and crank the tabletop together. Have a friend hold the nut on the rod with locking pliers at one end and use a ratchet wrench at the other end to tighten down the nut. Start at one end and work your way to the other, progressively squeezing it together. Use ratchet straps or clamps to facilitate this process, if necessary. Move as quickly as possible to make sure the center seam is tight before the glue starts to dry.

11 **Run the ¾" rods** through the holes near the feet, placing two washers between the legs in each pair and one washer and one nut on the outside of each leg. Tighten everything down, using the nuts to adjust the legs so that they are roughly the same width apart at the bottom as they are at the top. Since each pair of legs will be cinched together at the bottom, they will splay slightly as you tighten down the threaded rods. This spreading effect helps widen the base and make the table more stable.

12 **Trim off any excess threaded rod** with a hacksaw or an angle grinder.

13 **Build up one more strip** down each side, counterboring it first to surround the exposed ends of the threaded rods, nuts, and washers. This will make the nuts flush into the sides of the table for a finished appearance. Keep in mind the screw heads will be exposed down the sides, so position them neatly.

14 **Find the center of the trestles** and make a mark on the top of the tabletop. Measuring out from the center, draw two lines at equal distances from the center, one at each end. Trim the wild ends off flush with a circular saw and straightedge guide.

15 **Use the block plane and belt sander** to flush the surface of the table. Ease all the edges with a sanding block to ward off splinters. Start with 80-grit belt, then move up to a 100-grit. Switch to an orbital sander at 120-grit to polish the final surface.

16 **Seal the table** with your favorite finish, building up several coats on the top. This table is a good candidate for any sort of wipe-on oil finish (see page 62), which will soak into the dissimilar woods and not crack as the pieces expand and contract over time.

DISPOSAL *This table is very difficult to take apart. If it has outlived its usefulness as a large table, trim off the legs and install as a countertop, or cut up with a circular saw and make smaller tables. Donate to Goodwill, a friend, or relative.*

BRACKET CHAIR

Chairs are difficult objects. The ergonomics are pesky and the structural loads complex, requiring head-scratching joinery and quality materials. Chairs are also the most fundamental pieces of furniture, instantly turning a bare space into a proper room. The Bracket Chair aspires to be a universal chair system that can be adapted to whatever materials are on hand. Instead of designing the whole form, I concentrated only on the joints, locking them into place with triangular arrangements of mending plates. The plates are available in many forms at the hardware store, from cheap galvanized strips to nice stainless-steel bars. Any kind of mismatched wood can be used, even if it varies somewhat in width.

MATERIALS

- Ten wood strips (preferably hardwood), ¾" thick × 18" long and at least 1½" wide
- 2½" #6 wood screws
- Sixteen 4" mending plates
- ¾" #6 wood screws
- Two pieces ¾" plywood, 16" × 16", or several strips at least 16" long whose widths add up to 32"
- Finish of your choice
- Cushion material (closed-cell foam and canvas; optional)

TOOLS

- Pencil
- Tape measure
- Miter saw
- Drill/driver
- Square
- Circular saw

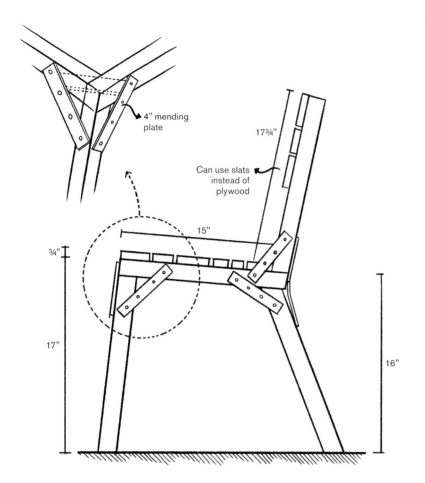

4" mending plate

17¾"

Can use slats instead of plywood

15"

¾"

17"

16"

CUT LIST

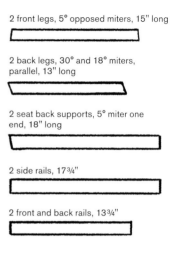

2 front legs, 5° opposed miters, 15" long

2 back legs, 30° and 18° miters, parallel, 13" long

2 seat back supports, 5° miter one end, 18" long

2 side rails, 17¾"

2 front and back rails, 13¾"

TIP With a pile of scrap slats and a stop-block setup, it is easy to manufacture parts for multiple chairs relatively quickly. This example is made of maple salvaged from an old bookcase; poplar door casings, oak cabinet face frames, or even old hardwood flooring are also good candidates.

STEPS

1 **Cut two front legs** at 15" long, with 5-degree opposed miters on the ends. Pull your measurement from long side to long side of the miters.

2 **Cut two back legs** with a 30-degree miter at one end and an 18-degree miter at the other, roughly parallel to one another. The piece should be 12¾" on the short side and 13" on the long side.

3 **Cut two seat back supports** to 18", with a 5-degree miter in one end only.

4 **Cut two side seat rails** to 17¾", with square ends. Cut a front and a back seat rail to 13¾", also with square ends.

5 **Assemble the seat frame** by screwing through the side rails and into the front and back seat rails with 2½" wood screws; be sure to predrill to prevent splitting. Confirm the seat frame is square, then put a mending plate across the bottom of each corner, using ¾" screws, so that the plate forms the hypotenuse of a 45-45-90 right triangle.

6 **Pocket-screw the back supports** into the side rails of the seat frame by predrilling down at an angle, aligning the back of each back support to the back edge of the seat frame. The seat back supports should be fastened through their mitered end, creating an ergonomic tilt to

the back. Start the drill bit perpendicular to the wood; once the bit is "seated," slowly rotate the drill up to the desired angle and drive forward. Pocket-drilling is a good way to snap drill bits and split wood, so *go slowly*.

7 **Strap the back supports** to the frame with two mending plates each. The plates should come off the back supports at visually congruent angles, as shown.

8 **Repeat the process for the legs.** Flip the chair over and pocket-screw the front legs, making sure the long edge of each leg is facing forward. Strap the legs into place with the mending plates. The short edge of the back legs should face backward, pocket-screwed through the 30-degree miter. Strap the back legs in place. The back straps will bend, due to the conflicting angles of the seat frame and the back leg — a little bending is fine, as long as the straps draw tight to the wood at each end.

9 **Stand the chair upright.** Create seat and backrest surfaces with two pieces of plywood or a number of slats, screwing them at their ends to the seat frame and back supports.

10 **Finish the chair** and add cushions as desired. This is meant to be a rough and quick chair, so I finished mine only with wax.

DISPOSAL *With no glue or permanent joinery, this chair can be broken back into parts. Recycle the wood, plates, and screws into other projects, or compost or burn the wood. Throw out the plywood.*

TIP You can adapt the basic strategy at work in the bracket chair — triangulating joints with metal straps — to a wide variety of pieces. Experiment with tables, shelves, or different chair geometries.

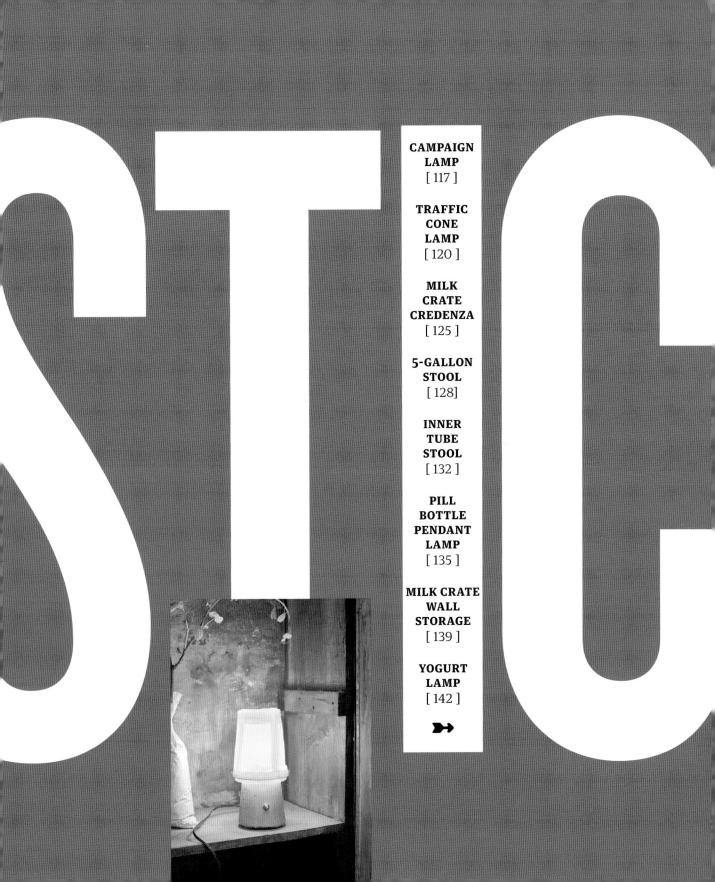

STIC

PLASTIC IS A CONTRADICTORY MATERIAL. LIGHT, BUT DENSE. THIN, BUT STRONG.

Durable, but disposable. Recyclable, but made from fossil fuels. Modern polymers, produced from petrochemicals, are energy-intensive to produce and last literally *forever*, but we toss them out without a second thought. Recycling is helpful, but it can't eliminate the enormous amounts of atmospheric plastic, corroded bits and pieces that are in the air, soil, and oceans. There is an opportunity inside these paradoxes: plastic is cheap and tough, and using it for furniture keeps it out of our environment.

The first modern plastic was unveiled at the 1862 Great International Exhibition in London by Alexander Parkes. Made of green cellulose, the wonder material was transparent, moldable, and ultimately unprofitable. A few years later, cellulose came to market, an organic material made from cotton and camphor. It was mostly used as a substitute for ivory in the manufacture of billiard balls. In 1907, Leo Baekeland invented his eponymous Bakelite, the first completely synthetic plastic. A mixture of phenol and formaldehyde, Bakelite ushered in an era of modern consumer goods made from molded or extruded plastic. It also introduced the public

to this new class of synthetic products, shaped into abstract forms for abstract tasks — radios, telephones, electrical insulators.

From the mid-1920s until the mid-1950s, plastics were a growth industry. PVC (used for sewage pipes) was born in 1920, followed by polyethylene (plastic bags) in 1933, Teflon (nonstick pans) in 1938, nylon (stockings) in 1939, ABS (Legos) in 1948, polyester (clothing) in 1951, and Styrofoam (takeout trays) in 1954. Early manufacturing processes were often toxic, and the legacy of this production spree is written all over the industrial cities of America. Plastics are very new, in a historical sense, and safety issues continue to crop up as these materials mature. BPA (bisphenol A) has been around since 1957, but concerns about its ability to mimic hormones in the human body came to light only in the last few years. Companies are now returning to organically derived formulas in hopes of creating biodegradable, sustainable substitutes.

Plastic is so durable it might as well be immortal, but we use it for temporary products. Milk crates, grocery carts, 5-gallon buckets, soda bottles, and those damned tree-stuck grocery bags are so common as to be invisible. Other cheap products of the consumer-industrial complex — tires, inner tubes, nylon webbing — can be adapted into new uses, bought with plastic cards and turned into ad-hoc furniture. The keen-eyed guerilla can quickly forage enough parts for several of the projects in this section; others require patient accumulation of household materials like bottles and bags. Many of the projects in this section are lamps, as plastic is particularly suited to diffusing light.

MATERIALS

PILL BOTTLES

Based on a 2008 report by the Centers for Disease Control, it's safe to assume that about 47 percent of Americans took at least one prescription drug in the last month. That rounds out to about 147 million people, a lot of pills and a lot of bottles to hold them. Pill bottles are usually orange, varying widely in material: PET (polyethylene terephthalate), LDPE (low-density polyethylene), HDPE (high-density polyethylene), or PVC (polyvinyl chloride), all of which are petroleum-derived plastics. Modular in shape and size, they have good lids and a pleasant translucency to them. Collect them from elderly relatives, or put up a post on social media asking folks to save their old ones for you. Once a pile has been accumulated, go through and remove the labels by soaking in hot water, then use a citrus-based de-gummer to get the glue residue off.

PLASTIC BOTTLES

Just about every liquid we consume — milk, water, soda — comes to us in a plastic bottle. Milk jugs are made from HDPE (high-density polyethylene), which is resilient and flexible. The squared-off shape of the jugs also makes it easier to extract useful panels from their walls. Water and soda bottles are typically made from PET (polyethylene terephthalate), which is cheaper and more brittle than HDPE. They have little structural strength and are typically in molded, tinted shapes that make them difficult to adapt to projects. However, they make interesting forms for concrete and are easy to peel away once the mix has cured.

PLASTIC BAGS

When first introduced in the 1950s, plastic bags were seen as a great advance — cheaper, stronger, and easier to carry than paper versions. However, light and wind-blown, they have matured into a disposal nightmare. Many cities have introduced bag taxes or bans to discourage their use, but as many as one trillion are still manufactured every year. Most are used once and then thrown out; the EPA estimates fewer than one percent are recycled. Made of gossamer-thin PET, plastic bags can be recycled by being cut, molded, and welded together. Similar manufacturing techniques can be adapted for home use by the guerilla, by fusing together multiple layers of bags using a household iron (see Fusing Plastic Bags on page 113). The resulting fabric is great for lampshades, bags, book covers, and window shades, but it's not strong enough for load-bearing applications.

TYVEK

Tyvek is a flexible, fabric-like plastic made from spun HDPE fibers. Tough and puncture-resistant, it is used mostly for postal envelopes, packaging, disposable paint suits, and as house wrap. The unique weave allows one-way transport of water, permitting vapor to penetrate the pore structure in one direction, but blocking liquid water droplets in the other direction. This allows the house to breathe, exhaling interior humidity while locking out the weather. Usable scraps are usually plentiful in construction dumpsters. Tyvek can be worked with a sewing machine. Use for hammocks, sling chairs, and lampshades.

CORRUGATED PLASTIC

Corrugated plastic (often referred to by the brand name Coroplast) is made of two thin sheets of polypropylene with a fluted layer in between, forming a stiff, chemical-resistant board. Many of the same tools and techniques used with corrugated cardboard apply to its plastic cousin, except it is difficult to glue. 3M makes a specialty adhesive for polypropylene, or it can be heat-welded. Mechanical fasteners – screws, rivets, and machine bolts – work well, paired with washers to prevent tear-through. The simplest method is slot-and-tab retention, which can be done very precisely with this clean-cutting plastic material. Commonly used for political yard signs and other temporary advertisements, corrugated plastic is available in bulk during election season and is fairly cheap otherwise.

MILK CRATES

Milk crates are the urban guerilla's best friend: modular, stackable, sturdy, and available everywhere. However, distributors own crates, and those stacks of empties behind convenience stores and restaurants are not free for the taking. Crates can be found all over cities, in alleys, ravines, storm sewers, abandoned buildings, yard sales, and secondhand stores. My personal rule is to only take crates not in the discernable vicinity of a restaurant or grocery store. As a last resort, a number of online retailers will sell new crates for around $10 apiece. Make sure you are getting genuine,

heavy-duty commercial crates and not flimsy big-box-store knockoffs.

Milk crates are made from PET, injection-molded into a rigid grid structure to make stiff, interlocking boxes. However, if you cut into a crate and interrupt the latticework, the unit begins to lose strength, proportional to the amount of lattice removed. The heavy-duty plastic takes conventional fasteners well, including drywall screws and through-bolts. The lattice structure also lends itself to tying together with zip ties, which is a quick and tool-free option. An angle grinder, rotary tool, or hacksaw will cleanly cut through plastic crate material.

5-GALLON BUCKETS

Commonly used for paint and drywall compound, 5-gallon buckets are made from PET with a wire bail. Look for empties in dumpsters outside jobsites or in alleyways, as well as orphans in vacant lots. In the restaurant industry, lots of ingredients – sauces, syrups, oils, shortenings, icings – come packaged in 5-gallon buckets, but the cleanup time may not be worth it. Clean found buckets very thoroughly. Graphics can be removed with acetone or fine-grit sandpaper. Lacking salvage, you can buy buckets at most home centers for five or six bucks, with or without lids. Similar to milk crates, 5-gallon pails can be screwed and bolted and are easy to cut with an angle grinder.

PVC PIPE

PVC (polyvinyl chloride) has become ubiquitous, used in everything from inflatable pool toys to sewage pipes. It is strong but brittle, especially in cold weather. When exposed to UV light for prolonged periods, PVC can discolor and become prone to impact breakage. It has been approved for both water supply and drainage lines in the U.S., but some European countries still ban its use for supply lines due to concerns over leaching of phthalates into drinking water.

PVC is easy to work, cutting with a conventional miter saw or a hacksaw. The dust and filings are statically charged, which can make cleanup a chore. In construction applications, PVC is chemically welded together with various fittings, using a two-part (primer and epoxy) glue system to create a leakproof joint. Basic off-the-shelf fittings include elbows (commonly available in 22.5-, 30-, 45-, and 90-degree angles), pipe caps, and straight couplings for joining two lengths of pipe in a straight line. Alternatively, joints can be simply butted, with a wood dowel insert that spans both pipes, pinned in place with a drywall screw.

PVC can be bent if softened with a heat gun (do this carefully and in a *well-ventilated* area). To help prevent kinking, you can temporarily cap the pipe and fill it with sand or water prior to heating. PVC pipe is extremely cheap, and most home centers will cut pipes to length for you; however, check with the salesperson to see if they charge by the foot or for the whole piece before you put saw to plastic. The printing on the outside of the pipe can be removed with acetone or with fine-grit sandpaper. Heavier sanding can take off the shine, dulling the pipe to a matte, bone-like finish.

RUBBER

Rubber, one of the original industrial plastics, is a natural compound. Its manufacture begins by harvesting latex from slashes in the bark of rubber trees. The ancient Olmecs used this natural rubber to make game balls and simple footwear. Discovered by European colonists, rubber trees were then disseminated to India, the Belgian Congo, and other subtropical climates and plantation-farmed. In 1839, Charles Goodyear invented vulcanization, heating raw rubber with sulfur, bisphenol, and peroxide to improve durability and resilience. Today, over half of rubber products are produced synthetically from petroleum by-products, which is what makes old tire dumps so flammable.

Rubber is available to the guerilla in a number of ready-made forms, mostly inner tubes, tires, and hoses. Old air hoses for pneumatic tools, typically ⅜" in diameter, are strong and resilient and make a very comfortable surface for woven seating. Inner tubes, available in every conceivable size online, can be inflated into simple seats, or woven flat into surfaces. Rubber can be cut with a sharp utility knife and joined with machine bolts, drywall screws, or by sewing with an awl and a heavy needle.

Fusing Plastic Bags

Lay a piece of parchment paper on a flat, heat-resistant surface. Add two plastic grocery bags, cut and unfolded, then top the stack with another piece of parchment paper. Run over your sandwich with an iron set on low (nylon/synthetic) heat, starting in the center and moving out to the edges with firm pressure. If the heat is set too high, little lacy holes will melt into the plastic. Once two are welded together, let them cool, then add more sheets, one at a time, until desired thickness is reached. Cut and sew (or weld) the finished material to shape.

NYLON

DuPont Laboratories first synthesized nylon in 1935. It shot to fame a few years later when it replaced silk in women's stockings during wartime. Extremely strong in tension, nylon was ideal for hosiery, jackets, webbing, and rope. Webbing has become widely used for backpacking gear, and a wide variety of accessory buckles and fittings are available online. Buckles are usually made from ABS plastic, but some are made from hard, molded nylon. Cut woven nylon can be fused with an open flame to prevent fraying, and then sewn with nylon thread and midsize needle. The guerilla can use webbing as tension straps to brace legs in tables and chairs; as assembly straps for flat-pack pieces; and, in the form of ratchet straps, as lightweight, portable clamps in the nomadic workshop. In rigid applications — small nuts, washers, buckles, toothbrushes, and combs — nylon is brittle and given to sudden failure, especially from impact.

ACRYLIC

Acrylic (methyl methacrylate) was first synthesized in 1928, concurrently discovered by a number of different scientists around the world.

Brought to market a few years later under the name Plexiglas, it was quickly put to use in everything from airplane canopies to contact lenses. Hardware stores now sell it by the sheet, in ⅛" and ¼" thicknesses. It can be cut with a circular saw or jigsaw, or with a table saw and a fine-toothed plastics blade. For straight cuts, you can also simply score the material and snap it over a hard edge. Acrylic is brittle and prone to cracking when cut and drilled, so go slowly. It can be joined with conventional superglue (cyanoacrylate), which reacts chemically with the plastic and melts it together like a weld. Gentle application of heat, either with a gun or an oven, makes acrylic flexible enough to bend or vacuum-form into complex shapes. Once the material cools, it will retain the new shape.

MELAMINE BOARD

Melamine is a thin laminate resin, usually applied over a particleboard core to make smooth sheet goods used in cabinets and casework. Dense, heavy, and flat, melamine board makes an excellent surface for molding concrete or resins. It can be worked like wood — use a laminate blade to keep the surface from chipping. The surface is impervious to moisture and many chemicals, but once cut the exposed particleboard edges must be protected by edge-banding, paint, or other finish.

CONCRETE

Concrete is a plastic material: a slurry that hardens into the shape of its container. First developed by the Romans, the recipe for concrete was lost to history in the Dark Ages. It was rediscovered in 1824 by Joseph Aspdin, a bricklayer on the English island of Portland who combined burnt (calcified) limestone and ground gypsum. When hydrated, the calcium compounds in cement undergo a pozzolanic reaction and cure to a stone-like density. Concrete is a mixture of one part cement, two parts sand, and three parts aggregate (typically gravel). Very strong in compression, concrete is weak in tension, vulnerable to cracking and impact damage. To prevent cracking, steel reinforcing bar or mesh is embedded into the wet mix. Long used in heavy construction, concrete is now used as interior finished floors, countertops, tabletops, and outdoor furniture. It is extremely inexpensive and fairly easy to work with, and it can be sealed with a simple water-based polyurethane.

TOOLS

BOX CUTTER

A sharp box cutter makes clean, smooth cuts in thin plastic sheeting of all kinds, including plastic bottles, Tyvek, and corrugated plastic. The relative slipperiness of the material can cause problems with keeping a straightedge aligned, so make sure to use a ruler with a rubber or cork backing, and tape down the material to keep it taut.

HACKSAW

A hacksaw is typically used to cut pipe, threaded rods, and other types of metal. It usually consists of U-shaped handle and a thin, fine-toothed straight blade. If cutting through something especially wide or deep, buy a hacksaw that's just a straight handle that holds a standard hacksaw blade, so the frame won't interfere with the cut. Available at any hardware store for just a few bucks, hacksaws make fine, clean cuts in plastics. The narrow, flexible blade makes it easy to maneuver around corners and into tight situations.

ROTARY TOOL

A rotary tool (commonly known by the brand name Dremel, although many manufacturers make similar tools) is basically a tiny router — a handheld, vertical-axis cutting and grinding tool that can accept a variety of attachments. Available in corded and battery-powered versions, the tool itself is fairly cheap, but the blades and bits are expensive and wear out quickly. Use cut-off wheels for nipping through milk crates and 5-gallon pails; use grinding attachments to de-burr and clean up cut edges; and use fine drill bits on low speeds to drill holes in brittle plastics like pill bottles.

ANGLE GRINDER

An angle grinder (see page 151) is a grown-up rotary tool, with a larger motor and disc attachments up to 6" in diameter. Usually used in metalworking, angle grinders fitted with a cutoff wheel make short work of cutting plastic. Most come with a blade guard that covers the spinning cutting edge and deflects sparks, but this guard also often interferes with cuts. If the guard is off, the angle grinder becomes a very dangerous machine. The rotary motion of the cutting disc lacks the ballast of a baseplate (unlike a router or circular saw), which makes the tool vulnerable to spinning, catching, and torqueing. Always wear gloves and safety glasses when using an angle grinder.

HEAT GUN

Heat guns are a lot like hair driers but with smaller fans and bigger heating elements. Using electricity to produce raw heat draws a lot of power, and it is easy to blow a breaker when running a heat gun at full blast. If possible, try to plug into an outlet with 20-amp service, keep an eye on the fuse box, use a heavy-duty extension cord, and never leave a heat gun unattended. Use a heat gun to gradually soften plastics for bending. Make sure to operate in a well-ventilated area.

SOLDERING IRON

A soldering iron is a heat gun condensed into a pencil point. Typically used for hobbyist electronics, the precision delivery of heat makes a soldering iron ideal for spot-welding or boring small, neat holes in plastics. However, most soldering irons have no intensity control, so moderation of heat is based solely on duration of contact. Use an iron only in a well-ventilated area. While working, periodically scrape residue off the tip to prevent it from building up and burning.

DRILL/DRIVER

When drilling plastics, use sharp bits, and run the drill slow, as most plastic is extremely soft and easily melted by hot bits. Be careful with acrylic or PET, as they are brittle and prone to shattering when drilled. Prevent cracking by drilling a small pilot hole and gradually enlarging it, drilling more slowly with each increase in bit size. The cutting edges of the larger bit tend to catch on the rim of the smaller hole, cracking the plastic; drilling slowly helps minimize this problem. Do not use the impact driver on brittle plastics, like pill bottles, as the hammering action of the driver bit may crack the material.

POP-RIVET GUN

A handheld rivet gun uses a simple lever system to tightly bind layers of material. It is generally used for ductwork and guttering, where blind, one-sided fastening is desirable. Rivets come in a variety of lengths, with a variety of different "grabs," or total thickness of material that they can fasten effectively. Choose the right length and grab for the plastic you are joining, drill a hole, insert the rivet, and pump the handle of the rivet gun until it pulls the rivet tight and snaps off the protruding pin. The addition of a washer under the rivet head will help prevent tear-through.

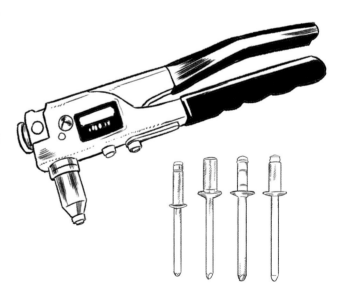

▲
POP-RIVET GUN Insert the long tail of the rivet into the head of the rivet gun and the short tip of the rivet into the pilot hole in the materials to be joined. Pump the handle until the material draws tight and the tail of the rivet snaps off.

METHODS

CUTTING

Dense, homogenous, and grainless, plastics can be cut with a variety of tools. The most basic tool is a box cutter with extendable, breakaway blades, good for everything from plastic bags to milk cartons. For milk crates, molded extrusions and harder plastics, a hacksaw works well.

As for power tools, rotary tools and angle grinders use cutoff wheels to make quick cuts, but may crack or shatter brittle plastics. Circular saws and table saws can be used to effectively cut sheet goods like Plexiglas, laminate, and melamine board. Be sure to use a plastic or laminate blade — lots of fine, hard teeth — to prevent chip-out and shattering. Laser-cutting is available online and at local hackerspaces. You will need some computer expertise to make the drawings, but the laser makes exceptionally clean cuts in acrylic, perfect for small, intricate pieces.

JOINING

Joining plastics can be tricky. Unlike most other materials in this book, the tools used to manipulate plastics on a commercial scale — vacuum pumps, casting machines, and plastic welders — are not available to the average consumer. However, there are workarounds to nearly everything.

Slot-and-tab joinery can be used well with sheet goods, namely corrugated plastic. Thinner plastic sheeting cuts cleanly and is durable enough to prevent tear-out around the edges of holes. Cut arrowhead-shaped tabs in one piece or side, then fold and join to the next piece by inserting the tab into a corresponding slot. The narrow neck of the arrowhead gets trapped in the slot and won't pull out.

Zip ties are a quick and cheap option for all-plastic joinery. Drill a small hole in adjoining pieces, then "sew" them together with a zip tie. Pull the tie tight with pliers and snip off the excess with wire snips. You can daisy-chain loops of ties (similar to making kids' paper chains) to make longer pieces.

Plastic glue comes in two basic types: solvent cements and reactive cements. Solvent cements work by melting the plastic a little bit, chemically welding the mating surfaces. Common types are the "purple" PVC cement and old-fashioned model airplane glue. Reactive cements are two-part epoxies, which rely on a resin and a catalyst that create a chemical reaction when mixed. Epoxies tend to be toxic and expensive, with a high-strength bond that isn't really necessary for most guerilla projects. For acrylic (Plexiglas), simple superglue will do the trick.

Conventional mechanical fasteners — drywall screws, rivets, or machine bolts — can be used with some plastics. Take care when drilling, as the bit can catch and crack the material with little warning. Use a small bit and go slow, then enlarge the hole with a bigger bit if needed. For screws, predrill and then fasten with a small washer (neoprene or rubber washers work well) under the head to distribute pressure and prevent cracking. For machine bolts, hold adjoining pieces together with spring clamps and drill through both with a slightly over-size bit. Use washers on both sides of the bolt and avoid overtightening.

MOLDING

Modern engineering has developed lots of industrial plastic molding techniques — injection, rotational, and 3-D depositional printing. Most of these are not available to the guerilla, though 3-D printing is becoming increasingly affordable. Some DIY methods of plastic molding have been kicked around the Internet, but they are fairly crude compared with commercial results.

In the context of this book, molding refers to concrete pieces. The simplest mold is an existing container. Plastic vessels — takeout containers, milk jugs, yogurt tubs — make great formwork, as their tapered forms and smooth sides make for an easy mold release. Since plastic is impervious, moisture can escape from the curing concrete only through the opening of the container, retarding curing. Slow curing is not a bad thing, as it strengthens the end product.

CAMPAIGN LAMP

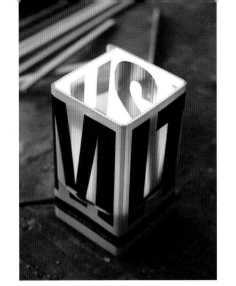

Every four years, the U.S. lurches through a bout of political combat. Punch-drunk cable news anchors swipe at bright maps, explaining demographics. Campaign ads blanket the airwaves. And then, in the blink of an eye, it's all over, leaving millions of signs studding yards like wreckage on the field of battle. The Campaign Lamp slices up a few scraps of sign, slotting them together without any fasteners. Lighted by a ready-made fixture, the reassembled graphics are stripped of their context and given new life as a fresh bedside lamp.

MATERIALS

- One corrugated plastic campaign sign
- One 4" studio lamp with aluminum shade
- One CFL or LED light bulb (wattage of your choice)

TOOLS

- Ruler or tape measure
- Permanent marker
- Straightedge
- Box cutter

STEPS

1 **Cut a panel of sign material** 12" high by 26" long. Make sure the corrugations run parallel to the 12" sides.

2 **Lay out the lamp sides** on what will be the inside of the completed lamp: Draw lines to divide the panel into four rectangles 6" wide, leaving a 1" strip on each end, as shown on next page. Mark a line 4" up from the bottom all the way across the panel. Mark out three arrowheads on one of the 1" side strips as shown. Mark three corresponding slots on the other side.

3 **Cut out the slots and arrowheads.** Cut four ⅛"-wide slots centered over your 4" line, each slot centered side to side in its respective rectangle. Carefully score along all your vertical lines, cutting through the face layer of the sign only — again, on the inside face of the panel.

4 **Mark a 5⅞" square** on a leftover piece of sign material, to create the baseplate. Draw a shallow point centered along each side of the square, as shown on next page. Cut out the points, then notch each corner with a pair of ½"-long × ⅛"-wide slots. Trace the socket of the lamp onto

PANEL TEMPLATE

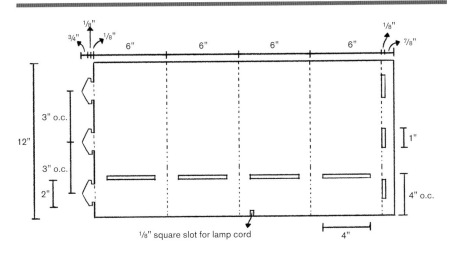

1/8"
3/4" 1/8"
6" 6" 6" 6"
1/8"
7/8"

12"

3" o.c.

3" o.c.

2"

1"

4" o.c.

1/8" square slot for lamp cord

4"

BASEPLATE

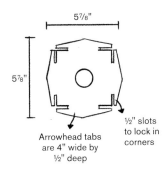

5 7/8"

5 7/8"

1/2" slots to lock in corners

Arrowhead tabs are 4" wide by 1/2" deep

FOLDING DIAGRAMS

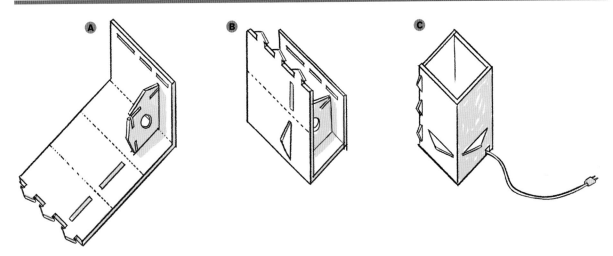

Ⓐ Ⓑ Ⓒ

the center of the baseplate and cut out, keeping the knife a little inside the marked circle for a tight fit.

5 **Insert an arrow of the baseplate** into the slot of one of the middle rectangles of the lamp panel. Make sure the scored side of the panel is facing up, so all your cut marks will be hidden once the lamp is complete. Fold up each side, fitting arrow tabs into slots.

6 **Remove the shade** from the studio lamp (see step 4 of the Cube Lamp on page 33). Put a

bulb into the baseplate from above, and the socket from below, sandwiching the baseplate in between. Cut a little 1/8"-square slot in the center of the bottom of one side for the cord to snake through.

Note: *Use only CFL (compact fluorescent) or LED light bulbs in this lamp; standard incandescent bulbs run too hot and may create a fire hazard.*

DISPOSAL *Disassemble and recycle plastic. Reuse electrical parts in a future project.*

TRAFFIC CONE LAMP

MATERIALS

- One traffic cone
- One piece ¾" plywood, approximately 16" square
- Paint or other finish of your choice
- Two all-weather rubberized light sockets
- Two CFL or LED light bulbs, 60W equivalent
- One medium-duty lamp cord, 8 to 12 feet long
- Heat-shrink tubing, ¼" diameter
- One toggle switch
- Solder
- Electrical tape
- One aluminum can
- One 1½"-diameter × 2" PVC pipe
- Duct tape
- Four ½" sheet metal screws
- Four ¾" × 6" carriage bolts
- Four #10 machine-bolt washers
- Four ¾" wing nuts
- Four ¾" hex nuts
- Eight ¾" washers

TOOLS

- Fan
- Soldering iron
- Pencil
- Tape measure
- Circular saw
- Sandpaper, 100-grit
- Drill/driver and ⅜", ¾", and 1¼" bits (plus smaller bits as desired)
- Clamps
- Wire strippers
- Lighter
- Scissors
- Dry-erase marker
- Box cutter
- Square
- Needle-nose pliers
- Wrench

Traffic cones are much abused, oft abandoned, and rarely thanked. It is easy to find one in half-decent shape, caught up in a storm grate or an urban ravine.

The Traffic Cone Lamp rescues an abandoned cone, cleans it up, perforates it, and mounts a light inside to create a Euclidean living room companion. Standing on small legs, with a switch atop its nose, it glows with a warm, comforting light. When necessary, drag it outside in winter to save that freshly shoveled curbside spot.

STEPS

1 **Wash the cone thoroughly,** inside and out, with hot soapy water.

2 **Set up the cone** in a well-ventilated outdoor area with the fan pointed directly at it. Use the soldering iron to melt holes in the rubber wall of the cone, pushing all the way through for full

holes or partway in for translucent depressions. Black rings of melted latex will build up around each hole — let them cool and harden in place, then cut off with a box cutter or putty knife. The holes may be punched in any pattern — I used a random distribution that fades in frequency toward the top. Set the cone aside.

3 Cut the plywood to the same dimensions as the base of the cone, typically about 14¾" for a full-size traffic cone.

4 Drill a radial pattern (or whatever pattern you prefer) of holes in the plywood base, making sure the center hole is at least 1¼" in diameter so the plug and cord can pass through.

5 Clamp the cone to the plywood, making sure all the edges and corners are aligned. Drill a ¾" hole in each corner, 2" in from each edge, through both the cone and the plywood. Sand the plywood and finish as desired.

6 Wire the two light sockets into the lamp cord — one at the end and one about 8" from the end. Strip the leads at the end of the lamp cord and slip a piece of heat-shrink tubing over each exposed lead, pushing it farther down the cord and out of the way. Tightly twist one lead (usually simple lamp cords do not differentiate their leads as "positive" or "negative," so just pick one) onto the white lead from one of the light sockets with needle-nose pliers. Repeat for the black lead. Slide the heat-shrink tubing over the exposed wires and shrink down with a lighter (run the lighter near — but not touching — the tubing, and it will shrink down around the wire). Measure 8" up from the end of the socket and cut the lamp cord. Strip the wires on both sides of the cut and wire in the second socket in the same manner as the first. Plug in and test; if the light fails, it probably means the second socket has its positive and negatives reversed.

7 Wire the toggle switch into the cord about 6" from the top light socket by cutting one of the wires in the lamp cord, stripping the two ends, and twisting them onto the two metal tabs on the underside of the toggle switch. Solder the connections and cover with electrical tape. Alternatively, if the switch has wire leads, twist the wires together and seal with heat-shrink tubing.

8 Cut off the bottom of the aluminum can with scissors to harvest the bottom and 2" of the attached side wall. Cut a series of vertical slits in the side wall, then bend and fold the strips

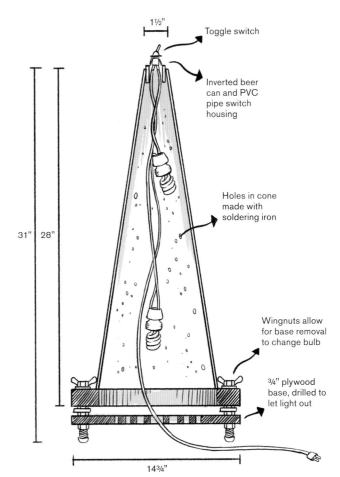

Toggle switch

Inverted beer can and PVC pipe switch housing

Holes in cone made with soldering iron

Wingnuts allow for base removal to change bulb

¾" plywood base, drilled to let light out

1½"

31" 28"

14¾"

TIP You can easily adapt the traffic cone lamp to desk size by using a 12" cone, one bulb, and no base plate. Experiment with LED bulbs and battery packs to make cord-free versions, perfect for outdoor parties.

down, turning the can inside out to create a dome. Drill a ⅜" hole in the center of the bottom of the can.

9 Unscrew the jam nut around the base of the toggle switch, push the base up through the hole in the can dome, then screw the nut on the top side of the dome, sandwiching the dome between the nut and the switch and securing the socket assembly to the can. Feed the wiring through the scrap of PVC pipe and push the pipe up snug to the underside of the can, with the strips of the can going around the outside of the pipe. Tape the can strips to the pipe with duct tape, wrapping it very tightly.

10 **Cut off the top 2" of the cone** with a box cutter. Push the switch/can assembly up into the top end of the cone. Predrill and screw through the cone into the pipe with four ½" sheet metal screws to secure, using washers under the screw heads so they don't tear through the cone.

11 **Install CFL (compact fluorescent)** or LED bulbs in the light sockets.

Note: *Do not use standard incandescent light bulbs, which run too hot and may create a fire hazard.*

12 **Attach the plywood base** to the cone with a carriage bolt in each corner, head-down. Put a nut and washer on the bolt and twist down the nut about 4". Put on the plywood base, followed by the cone, then add a washer and wing nut to each bolt. Twist each wing nut finger-tight, then bring up the bottom nuts until the whole lamp sits evenly and slightly elevated, with the lamp cord fed down through the center hole in the baseplate.

DISPOSAL *Strip out and recycle the electrical parts. Reuse the carriage bolts and traffic cone. Throw out the plywood.*

WIRING DETAILS

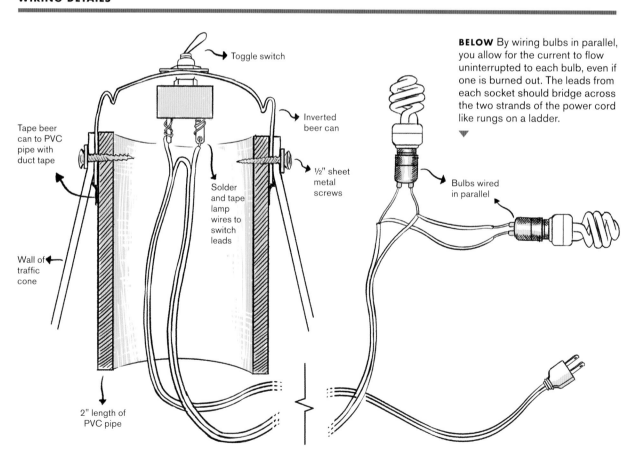

Toggle switch

Inverted beer can

Tape beer can to PVC pipe with duct tape

½" sheet metal screws

Solder and tape lamp wires to switch leads

Wall of traffic cone

2" length of PVC pipe

BELOW By wiring bulbs in parallel, you allow for the current to flow uninterrupted to each bulb, even if one is burned out. The leads from each socket should bridge across the two strands of the power cord like rungs on a ladder.

Bulbs wired in parallel

MILK CRATE CREDENZA

Milk crates are stout enough to carry about 33 pounds of milk. That's 64 pint-size cartons or 4 gallon jugs at 8.4 pounds apiece. The key to that strength is a diamond-grid structure, which eliminates weight while retaining rigidity. But, as the great modernists of the fifties taught us, a grid lives to be deformed.

The Milk Crate Credenza ties four crates together with zip ties, unifying with a sleek wood top. One more crate is cut and reassembled into a set of legs, adding a touch of class to ready-made street furniture. The crates serve as storage, while the smooth top provides a place to sit while putting on or taking off shoes.

MATERIALS

- Scrap wood, ¾" thick, at least 11" long
- One 52½" 1×12 (or plywood, 11¼" × 52½")
- Wood glue
- 1" drywall screws
- Finish of your choice
- Five milk crates
- Zip ties

TOOLS

- Pencil/permanent marker
- Tape measure
- Square
- Wood saw
- Drill/driver and ¼" bit
- Hand plane or 100-grit sanding block
- Spring clamps
- Needle-nose pliers
- Wire nippers
- Angle grinder, rotary tool, or hacksaw

STEPS

1 **Cut four strips of wood,** ¾" × ¾" × 10". Drill three ¼" holes through each strip for the zip ties, about 1" in from each end and in the center. Glue and screw the strips to the underside of the 1×12, spacing them 6½" in from each end and 13" on-center in between.

2 **Ease the edges** of the 1×12 top with a hand plane or sanding block. Sand and finish the top as desired.

3 **Create the leg assemblies** by cutting one crate as shown at right, severing a side and 4" of the bottom of the crate. Since the crates in the credenza are turned sideways (and are not perfect cubes), the legs must contract about 2" to match the width of the crates' sides. Slice down the middle of the leg crate, cut away the gridding, then slide the two halves past one another until the total unit is 11" long. Hold the two pieces together with spring clamps, drill through with a ¼" bit, then "sew" the pieces together with zip ties. Tighten up the ties with needle-nose pliers, and trim the

excess with wire nippers. Repeat the process to create a second leg assembly.

4 **Attach the four remaining crates together** with spring clamps, making sure they are flush and tight to one another. Drill through the front edge of each adjoining pair at the top and bottom, then attach with zip ties. Repeat along the back until the crates form a solid unit.

5 **Attach the wooden top** to the crates the same way, threading the zip ties though the holes drilled in the ¾" strips on the underside of the top.

6 **Attach the legs** at the intersections of the first and second and the third and fourth crates with a lot of zip ties. Small machine bolts may make for a sturdier structural joint here, but it's more conceptually coherent if the whole structure remains plastic as much as possible.

DISPOSAL *Disassemble by snipping the zip ties. Reuse the crates or put them by the curb for other scavengers. Recycle the wood into another project, burn, or compost. Recycle the legs.*

LEG CONSTRUCTION

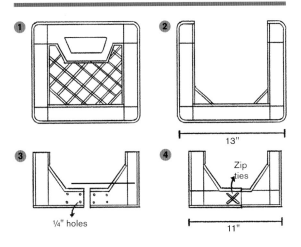

LEG ASSEMBLY

The leg assembly uses the strongest molded sections of the crates — the corners — contracted and stitched together into a sturdy U-shaped frame.

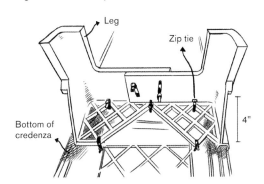

FRONT ELEVATION

SIDE ELEVATION

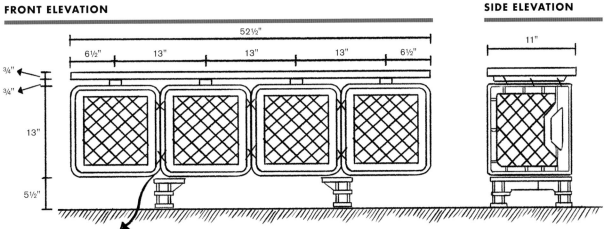

"Sew" adjoining crates together with zip ties

5-GALLON STOOL

Construction sites are littered with plastic buckets — 5-gallon pails that once stored paint or joint compound. The empties get flipped upside down, serving as natural stools at lunchtime.

The 5-Gallon Stool elevates this concept, lifting the bucket up on three tapering wooden legs. Near the base, the ridged rim of the bucket serves as a bottom brace and footrest. Scour jobsite dumpsters for empties, scraps of 2×4, and a few spare drywall screws, and this breakfast stool will cost you nothing but an afternoon.

MATERIALS

- One 5-gallon bucket
- Two 30" 2×4s
- 1" drywall screws
- 2½" drywall screws
- #10 washers
- Finish of your choice
- Acetone and steel wool (optional)

TOOLS

- Pencil
- Tape measure
- Miter saw
- Straightedge
- Circular saw
- Sandpaper, 100- and 120-grit
- Jigsaw
- Chisel
- Angle grinder or rotary tool
- Protractor
- Square
- Drill/driver and ⅛" bit

STEPS

1 Cut each 2×4 to 30" long, mitered 5 degrees at each end, in parallel.

2 Measure 1¼" in from one corner of each 2×4, along the mitered edge, and make a mark. Repeat at the opposite corner at the other end of the board. Connect the marks, forming a diagonal line (see template below). Cut with a circular saw to create the four leg blanks (you'll use only three).

3 Measure 8" up from the bottom of each leg, along the factory (untapered) edge, and make a mark. Mark a square line from the factory edge at the 8" mark, and measure ½" in along the square line. Measure 9¼" up from the bottom of each leg, along the factory edge. Connect the ½" and 9¼" marks, and cut out the resultant wedge with a jigsaw. Clean up the cut with a chisel and sandpaper as necessary.

4 Sand the legs and finish as desired.

5 Remove the lid and bail from the bucket. Clean thoroughly with hot soapy water. Use acetone and steel wool to remove graphics, if desired.

6 Use an angle grinder with a metal cut-off blade to cut the rim off the bucket (approximately the top 1¾"), being careful to keep the cut as straight as possible.

ELEVATION

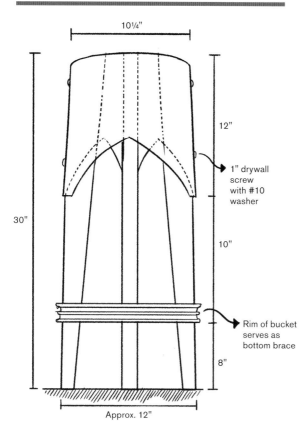

10¼"

12"

1" drywall screw with #10 washer

30"

10"

Rim of bucket serves as bottom brace

8"

Approx. 12"

LEG CUTTING TEMPLATE

Using tapered legs (a common technique used throughout this book) allows you to extract two legs from one piece of lumber for maximum material efficiency. Use 18" legs for a simple low stool that looks a little more elegant than a mere flipped-over bucket.

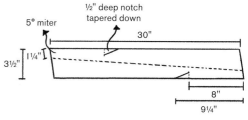

5° miter

½" deep notch tapered down

30"

3½"   1¼"

8"

9¼"

7 **Set a protractor** at the center of the bottom of the bucket. Make a mark every 60 degrees, as shown at right. Use a square to extend these lines down the sides of the bucket. Each line marks the centerline for a leg or the space between a leg. Mark three of the lines as "legs," and mark the other three lines as "spaces"; the leg lines and space lines should alternate. Measure ¾" to each side of each leg line along the cut edge of the bucket and make a mark. Measure 8" up from the cut edge along each space line. Connect the ¾" marks and the 8" marks with a sketched freehand arc. Once marked, cut out the three resultant arches with the grinder. Sand off any burrs on the plastic with 120-grit sandpaper.

8 **Set the cut bucket** on its bottom so the three plastic tabs are pointing up. Align one leg, factory edge out, with a "leg" centerline on one of the tabs. Confirm that the leg is square to the inside of the bottom of the bucket, and secure the leg with two or three 1" drywall screws with washers under their heads, predrilling with the ⅛" bit. Repeat for the remaining legs.

9 **Stand the stool up** and put one 2½" screw down through the bottom of the bucket and into the top of each leg.

10 **Slide the rim of the bucket down** over the stool until it fits into the leg notches. Make sure the stool is sitting evenly, then secure the rim with one or two screws at each leg.

11 **For comfort,** grind off the thin plastic ridges on the bottom of the bucket, which will dig into your thighs. Sand smooth. Be careful not to go all the way through the bucket.

DISPOSAL *Disassemble. Reuse, burn, or compost the wood. Recycle the bucket parts.*

MARKING BOTTOM OF BUCKET

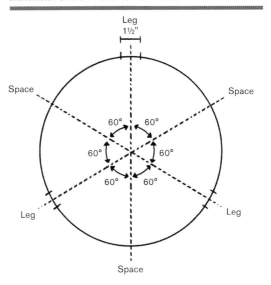

ARC CUTTING TEMPLATE

Use square to extend "leg" and "space" lines down bucket sides. Use a marker to sketch three 8-inch-high arches on the sides. Cut out the arches with an angle grinder.

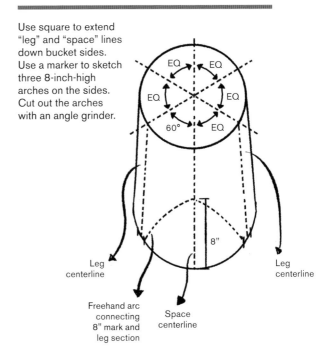

INNER TUBE STOOL

Summers in Alabama were hot, humid, and long. A few times a season, some friends and I would find our way to an old barn by a crook in the Cahaba River. You could rent a tube for a few bucks and float all day, piling into the back of a pickup to return to the start and begin again.

The Inner Tube Stool takes that essential, cushy comfort and mounts it to a flat-pack melamine-board base. Held together with nylon straps, the whole thing collapses in seconds. Make a batch and keep them tucked under the couch for unexpected guests, or take them down to a sandbar in the river, cast in a line, and crack a cold one.

MATERIALS

- Two pieces ¾" melamine board, 16" to 18" square
- One ¾"-wide × 96"-long nylon webbing strap
- One 13" ATV inner tube (or similar)
- Finish of your choice

TOOLS

- Pencil
- Tape measure
- Square
- Straightedge
- Circular saw (ideally with fine-tooth finish blade)
- Sandpaper, 100-grit
- File
- Drill and ¾" spade bit
- Router (optional)

PIECE A

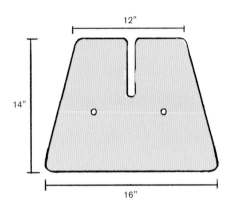

12"

14"

16"

PIECE B

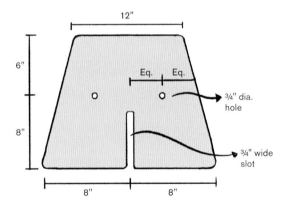

12"

6"

Eq.   Eq.

¾" dia.
hole

8"

¾" wide
slot

8"   8"

STRAPPING DIAGRAM

TIP The interlocking cruciform base can be adapted to other designs, supporting different stool or table tops. Instead of an inner tube, secure a flat panel on top by weaving a strap through eight 1-inch slots.

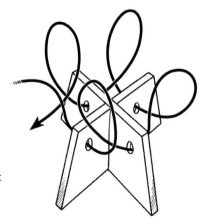

STEPS

1 **Lay out each half of the base** onto a square of melamine board, creating a trapezoid that's 14" tall and tapers from 12" wide at the top to 16" at the bottom. Cut out the base pieces with the circular saw.

2 **Draw a centerline,** top-to-bottom, on each base piece. Measure ⅜" to each side and draw a line parallel to the centerline; the outer lines represent the width of the notch for assembling the base pieces. Measure 6⅝" down from the top of one piece (piece A), and drill a ¾" hole, centered on the centerline. Measure up 6⅝" from the bottom on the other piece (piece B), and drill a ¾" hole, again on the centerline. Drill two more ¾" holes in each piece, 8" up from the bottom and centered between the centerline and the outer edges of the piece.

3 **Cut *just to the inside*** of each outer notch line, cutting down from the top of piece A to the ¾" hole; do the same to piece B, cutting up from the bottom. Test-fit the notches by fitting the pieces together at the notches, forming a cruciform shape when viewed from above.

4 **Disassemble the base** and ease the edges of the cut melamine with the file. I used a router with a roundover bit to clean up all the edges, but a thorough sanding also works just fine. Thoroughly sand all the particleboard visible at the cut edges, then wax, paint, or polyurethane the exposed wood surfaces. Particleboard absorbs moisture and swells, so take care that the edges are well sealed.

5 **Assemble the base.** Inflate the inner tube and place on top of the assembled base. Secure the base to the inner tube by weaving the nylon strap through the holes in the melamine pieces and up around the inner tube in a figure-eight pattern, as shown at left. Tighten the strap until the tube deforms a just a little bit.

DISPOSAL *Drop off the tube at a tire-recycling center, put the melamine in the general trash, and reuse the nylon strap around the house or in the car.*

PILL BOTTLE PENDANT LAMP

America is a prescription nation, with almost half of the population on some sort of medication. All those pills come in beautiful little bottles. Even if you are in perfect health, a few months of diligent collecting by friends and relatives could yield enough material for this project.

The Pill Bottle Pendant Lamp exploits the geometry of pill bottles, lassoing their necks with copper wire and pulling them tight to one another. The differential between the diameter of the neck and the diameter of the shoulders in each bottle will cause them to roll toward one another. Amass enough of them, and they assemble into a half-sphere, a geodesic spaceship for the living room.

MATERIALS

- At least 50 pill bottles, 3-month-supply size (approximately 1¾" diameter)
- Adhesive remover
- 100 feet 22-gauge copper craft wire
- One 20-foot medium-gauge orange extension cord
- ¼"- and ½"-diameter heat-shrink tubing
- One in-line switch
- One outdoor light socket with CFL or LED light bulb, 100W equivalent

TOOLS

- Wire strippers
- Crooked needle-nose pliers
- Standard needle-nose pliers
- Lighter
- Scissors

STEPS

1 **Wash and de-label all bottles** with hot soapy water. Remove adhesive residue with a gentle citrus-based adhesive remover. Let air-dry.

2 **Cut off a 24" piece of wire.** Loop one end tightly around the neck of one bottle, then twist it around itself to secure it in place. Secure the first bottle to two others by wrapping the necks in a figure-eight pattern. Pull the wire taut with the needle-nose pliers so the bottles tighten against one another, forming a tripod – group A – as shown.

3 **Create three pairs of bottles,** using 12" lengths of wire in a figure-eight pattern – group B – as shown. Attach one B pair to each bottle in the A grouping by looping around the neck of an A bottle and onto the wire link *between* the necks of the B pair. Use the crooked-nose pliers to get between the bottles of the B pair.

4 **Attach a single bottle (C)** into each of the three gaps between the B pairs by wiring around the neck of the C bottle and onto the wire link *between* the A bottles.

5 **Continue in this manner,** building up concentric rings of bottles on top of previous layers by adding a ring of B assemblies, then filling in the gaps with C bottles. Each ring will need more bottles than the last; the form eventually self-encloses into a half-dome as the shoulders of each bottle tighten against one another and the bottles curl upwards. Take care to keep the structure symmetrical as it grows.

6 **Cut the socket (female) end** off the extension cord with wire strippers. Peel back the outer insulation and strip the interior wires.

7 **Cut one segment** of ½" heat-shrink tubing to about 2" and feed it over the outside of the extension cord. Cut two segments of ¼" heat-shrink tubing and feed one over each of the black (hot) and white (neutral) cord wires.

GROUPS A AND B ASSEMBLIES

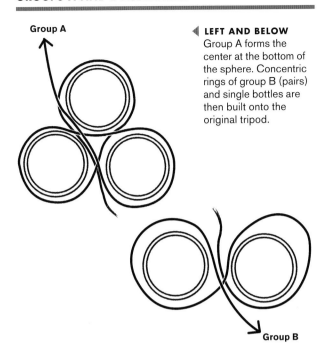

Group A

Group B

◀ LEFT AND BELOW
Group A forms the center at the bottom of the sphere. Concentric rings of group B (pairs) and single bottles are then built onto the original tripod.

LAMP ASSEMBLY

Once the first 12 bottles are in place, the symmetry and logic of additions will become self-evident.

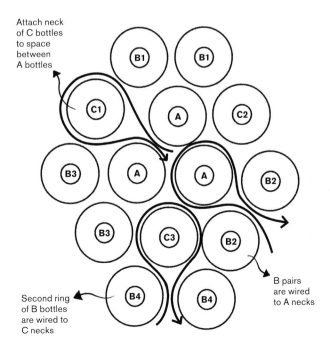

Attach neck of C bottles to space between A bottles

B pairs are wired to A necks

Second ring of B bottles are wired to C necks

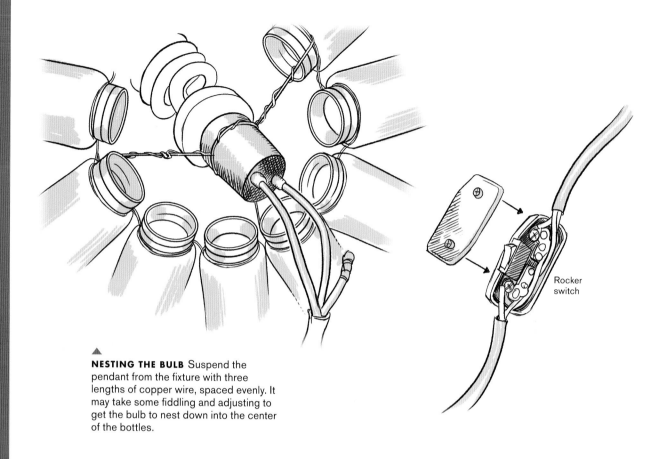

▲
NESTING THE BULB Suspend the pendant from the fixture with three lengths of copper wire, spaced evenly. It may take some fiddling and adjusting to get the bulb to nest down into the center of the bottles.

Rocker switch

8 **Twist the cord wires tightly together** with the leads from the outdoor light socket, matching the wire colors (black to black, white to white). Make sure the wires are securely twisted by tugging on them; since the fixture hangs from the cord, it's important that the connection be secure. Shrink the smaller bits of heat-shrink tubing over each individual connection so the bare wires won't touch one another. Run the lighter near (but not touching) the tubing, and it will shrink down around the wire. Slide up and shrink the bigger piece of tubing over the whole joint for a neat appearance.

Note: *If the socket fixture does not have a ground lead (typically green), cap off the extension cord's ground wire (also typically green) with heat-shrink tubing. The means the socket is not grounded, but this is common with simple light fixtures.*

9 **Install an in-line rocker switch** a few feet from the plug end of the cord, following the manufacturer's directions.

10 **Use three strands of wire** to secure the socket to the pendant so that the half-dome hangs evenly around the bulb. Suspend the fixture by the cord from an eyehook in the ceiling or mount on a wooden swing-arm.

Note: *Use only CFL (compact fluorescent) or LED light bulbs in this fixture; standard incandescent bulbs run too hot and may create a fire hazard.*

DISPOSAL *Disassemble and recycle parts.*

MILK CRATE WALL STORAGE

Milk crates are the oxen of the plastic world: stolid, unglamorous beasts of burden. They get kicked around in alleys and the backs of vans, hauling records and guitar pedals and serving as cigarette-break stools.

Milk Crate Wall Storage twists crates on the bias, adds some heavy-duty drywall anchors, and transforms these old reliables into an abstract wall creature. Arranging the crates on a 45-degree angle creates a self-reinforcing structure, where each box rests on its neighbor. Between crates, deep Vs are perfect for storing books and magazines. And, whenever you're ready to move, everything's already packed.

MATERIALS

- Six to ten milk crates
- Heavy-duty screw-type drywall anchors
- 2" #8 coarse-thread drywall screws
- #8 washers
- ¼"-thick hardboard or plywood, cut into 2" squares

TOOLS

- Pencil
- Tape measure
- Level
- Speed Square
- Drill/driver and ¼" bit

STEPS

1 Draw a level line on the wall, approximately 48" above the floor. Use the Speed Square to mark a line off that reference line, pointing down at 45 degrees.

2 Set your first crate aligned with the 45-degree line and with its corner just touching the level line. Drill a ¼" pilot hole through one of the openings in the bottom of the crate and into the drywall. Remove the crate and set an anchor at that point.

Note: *Use heavy-duty metal anchors that are shaped like threaded cones, with a minimum weight rating of 50 pounds.*

3 Reposition the crate and screw into the anchor with a drywall screw that has a washer and a 2" square of hardboard on it. The hardboard will act as large washer, distributing the holding power of the screw.

4 Add another anchor, somewhere lower in the crate.

5 Once the first crate is in place, the others should follow easily without measuring. Just register one crate against another, drill your pilot holes, and add the anchors. If there are large gaps between crates, due to warped plastic, hold them together along the mating using heavy-duty binder clips with the handles removed.

Note: *Make sure there's no wiring or plumbing in the wall where you drive your anchors. If you run into a wall stud when predrilling for anchors, stop drilling and simply drive the screw into the stud without using the anchor. If renting, ask the landlord before perforating the wall with a bunch of screw anchor holes (though they are easy to repair when you move).*

DISPOSAL *Remove crates and anchors from wall and patch holes with spackle. Most crates are made of recyclable plastic and can be cut up with a hacksaw into flat pieces and recycled. If not, set them out by the trashcan, and a scrapper will probably grab them.*

LAYOUT DIAGRAM

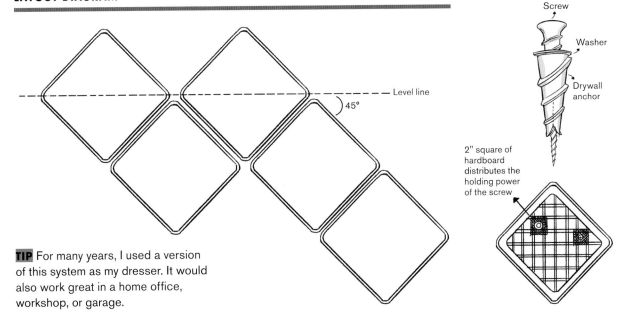

Level line

45°

Screw

Washer

Drywall anchor

2" square of hardboard distributes the holding power of the screw

TIP For many years, I used a version of this system as my dresser. It would also work great in a home office, workshop, or garage.

YOGURT LAMP

Yogurt usually comes in a sturdy tub, often reused as a poor man's Tupperware. The glossy sides and heavy-gauge plastic make yogurt containers ideal vessels for casting small pieces of concrete.

The Yogurt Lamp uses two matching containers, one as a mold for a concrete base and one as the support for the lampshade. All of the electrical parts are buried in the concrete, betrayed only by an old-fashioned metal push switch sticking out from the side. The shade is a simple sheath of welded grocery bags, sewn around a second yogurt container.

MATERIALS
- Two quart-size yogurt containers with lids
- One all-weather light socket
- One CFL light bulb, 60W equivalent
- One lamp cord
- 1/4" heat-shrink tubing
- One toggle switch
- 5-pound bucket of anchoring cement (a.k.a. nonshrink grout)
- Two gallon-size zip-top bags
- Electrical tape
- Two white plastic bags
- Parchment paper
- White thread or dental floss
- One wine cork (preferably synthetic)
- Construction adhesive or rubber model adhesive

TOOLS
- Drill/driver and 3/8" bit
- Craft knife
- Wire strippers
- Needle-nose pliers
- Lighter
- Scissors
- Iron
- Sewing needle
- Box cutter

BASE CASTING

Cast the base upside-down. Dimensions of the base may vary according to brand and volume. Let cure for several days to make sure it has hardened all the way through, then invert and remove the yogurt container.

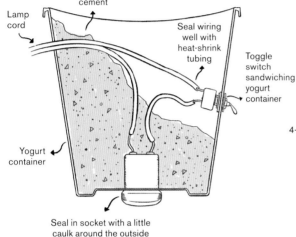

Lamp cord

Wet anchoring cement

Seal wiring well with heat-shrink tubing

Toggle switch sandwiching yogurt container

Yogurt container

Seal in socket with a little caulk around the outside

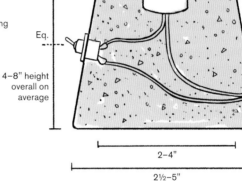

Yogurt tub lampshade

Yogurt lid

Eq.

4–8" height overall on average

2–4"

2½–5"

STEPS

1 **Drill a ⅜" hole** in the side of one yogurt container where you want the switch to be. Drill a second 3/8" hole on the opposite side of the container, near the rim, for the cord to pass through. Use the craft knife to cut another hole, centered in the bottom of the container, making it exactly the same diameter as the narrower part of the light socket. You want to be able to push the socket partway in so the top sticks out and the bottom (wire end) will be buried in the base.

2 **Separate and strip the ends** of the lamp cord. Push the ends of the wire through the 3/8" hole near the rim, leaving long leads to manipulate the wiring in the container. Push the socket through the hole in the base of the yogurt container. It should fit very tightly. Slide a piece of heat-shrink tubing down over each lead, past

the exposed wire. Twist one wire onto the white lead attached to the socket and the other wire to the black lead, using the needle-nose pliers to secure the connection. Slide the heat-shrink tubing back over the exposed wire and pass a lighter over it until it conforms tightly to the wire (run the lighter near – but not touching – the tubing, and it will shrink down around the wire). Snip one of the lamp cord wires and strip it. Slide a small piece of heat-shrink tubing over the wire on each side of the cut. Twist the leads onto the leads on the underside of the toggle switch, slide the heat shrink tubing over the exposed wire, and shrink it tight with the lighter. Pull out the excess length of wiring.

3 **Seal around the socket** on the outside of the container with a thin bead of caulk. (If you seal on the inside of the container, an unattractive line of caulk will end up embedded in the final product.) Take the jam nut off the base of the

LAMPSHADE SKELETON

The yogurt container lampshade skeleton attaches to a grocery bag "fabric" that casts a pleasant white light. Experiment with colored plastic bags for different effects.

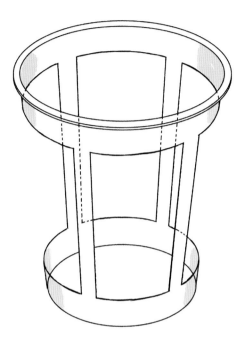

toggle switch, push it through the ⅜" hole on the side of the yogurt container, then screw the jam nut back on, securing the switch in place. Make sure the caulk has dried before proceeding to step 4.

4 **Mix the anchoring cement** by pouring some dry mix into a doubled zip-top bag, adding a little water, sealing and agitating with your hands. Make the mix as dry as possible while remaining workable, aiming for an oatmeal-like consistency. Pour the mix into the yogurt container, filling it up about ¼" to ½" shy of the rim. The container will now be balanced on the light socket, making it prone to tipping, so be careful to keep it balanced and upright. Once full, squeeze the sides of the container and poke the cement with a pencil or chopstick to work out any air bubbles. Let the cement cure for several days; don't remove the form even if the top looks dry.

5 **Cut four panels** out of the other yogurt container as shown, creating four thin ribs connecting the rim and the base. Cut a smaller concentric circle out of the bottom, ending up with a skeleton container. Cut a circle out of the center of the lid, slightly smaller than the diameter of the light bulb (again, CFL only) you are planning to use.

6 **Create a sheet of plastic-bag "fabric"** by cutting the bags open, laying them flat on top of one another between parchment paper, and ironing on low (see page 113). Move the iron slowly out from the center, trying to eliminate wrinkles. The bags should eventually fuse together into a single cohesive sheet.

7 **Sew the bag fabric** around the yogurt container skeleton with white thread or dental floss, creating one vertical seam where the fabric overlaps. Trim off excess at the top and the bottom, leaving about ½" of material on both ends. Secure the ½" excess flap by whip-stitching around the rim of the container, cinching the fabric down.

8 **Use a box cutter** to carefully slit and peel off the yogurt container from around the cement. Tape off the switch, and seal the cement with water-based polyurethane. Cut off three thin discs of wine cork and glue to the base of the lamp so the cement won't scratch tabletops.

9 **Flip the base right-side up** and add the light bulb. Carefully press the yogurt container lid onto the shade; it should just click into place, but since the shade has had so much material removed, it is no longer rigid enough to resist much pressure as you replace the lid. Screw the shade down onto the CFL, twisting the shade so that the hole in the center of the lid engages with the curlicue "threads" of the CFL tubing, resulting in the shade being held aloft.

DISPOSAL *Break up the cement base with a hammer and turn it back into gravel. Separate the electrical parts and plastic parts and recycle at an appropriate facility.*

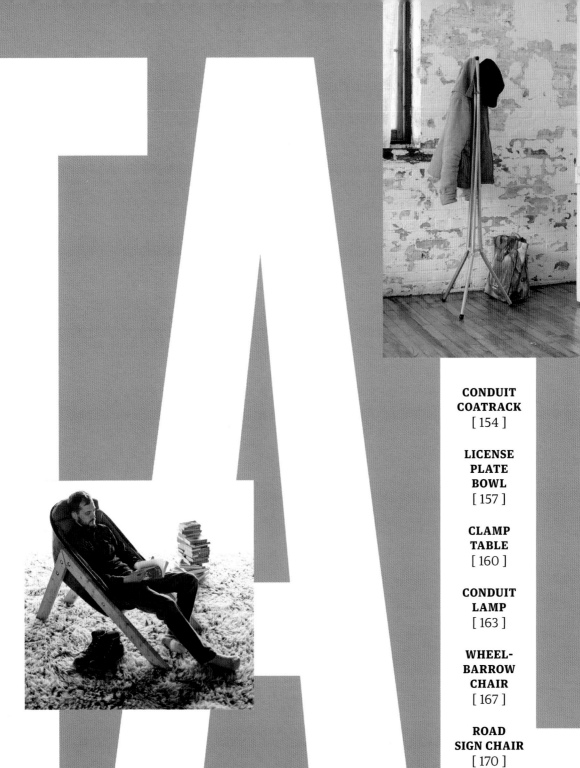

➤➤

METAL IS THE MOST ELEMENTAL OF MATERIALS BUT HARD TO RECOGNIZE IN THE NATURAL ENVIRONMENT.

Usually betrayed by oxidizing minerals — rust red or green copper — surface traces point to promising underground deposits. Prehistoric people exploited copper, gold, and other soft metals first, gradually acquiring the technology to mine and refine harder materials, like iron.

The Metals of Antiquity are the seven basic metals that were known to ancient peoples: gold, copper, silver, lead, tin, iron, and mercury. All of these metals, save iron, are relatively soft in their natural state, and are usually found in rocks that contain many other minerals and impurities. The first practical metal, copper, started being used around 6000 BC. Malachite, a green mineral that contains a large percentage of copper, was ground, smelted, and formed. Annealing, or controlled heating and cooling, helped harden the copper, but it was still too soft to make cutting edges. Mixing it with tin, however, produced a much harder (and easier to weaponize) alloy, bronze.

Iron was discovered long before people developed the technology necessary to make it useful.

Ore must be smelted at 1,100 degrees Celsius before it becomes flexible and resilient enough for forging. Clay furnaces and charcoal were able to develop the necessary heat, and wrought iron became the dominant material for tools and weapons. Cast iron began to be used in construction during the Victorian age, shaped into I-shaped cross-sections and riveted together into elegant long-span structures. For the first time, structure and skin were separated, allowing for much taller buildings and much bigger windows.

In 1855, Charles Bessemer patented a process for mass-producing steel, an alloy of iron and carbon. Closed furnaces smelted iron at very high temperatures, driving off impurities, and oxygen was pumped through the molten metal to oxidize it. Now, steel is produced in massive industrial quantities, a primary component in buildings, ships, and cars. Mid-century designers and architects — Le Corbusier, Mies van der Rohe, Eero Saarinen, Jean Prouvé, Marcel Breuer, Raymond Loewy — put steel into the domestic sphere, designing innovative furniture and houses out of a cold, industrial material.

Aluminum, as alum salts, makes up 8 percent of the Earth's crust, but it wasn't isolated into a solid metal until 1825, by Danish scientist Hans Christian Orstead. Remarkable for its light weight, high tensile strength, and corrosion resistance, aluminum also takes an enormous amount of energy to refine from its most common precursor, bauxite. However, it is infinitely recyclable without degradation in quality, making it very attractive to scrap dealers. Most commonly seen in beverage cans, it is also widely used for industrial components, bicycle parts, road signs, and architectural cladding.

Metal is widely available to the guerilla. Rising scrap prices and a difficult economy have made metal recycling a viable underground job again, and big cities all have their can men and alley-cat scrappers. The urban landscape is littered with signposts, signs, car parts, electrical conduit, piping, and the mass-produced fasteners that hold it all together. Every hardware store is a catalog of ready-made pieces, waiting to be combined into simple structures. The following projects are low-key, no-weld, introductory handshakes into the hard-edged world of metalworking.

MATERIALS

CONDUIT

Electrical conduit is used to house electrical wiring in buildings, protecting against damage and fire. The most common form, electrical metallic tubing (EMT), is a thin-walled galvanized steel pipe that is fairly cheap and easy to bend. Due to the galvanizing, it is relatively hard to cut and drill. While not designed to bear weight, EMT can be adapted to structural purposes by distributing load across multiple pieces. Temporary geodesic domes and tent structures have been made with EMT struts, ends flattened in a vise and drilled out to make simple bolt-through connections. Available cheaply at any hardware store, along with a host of standard fittings, conduit can also be recovered from dumpsters and on construction sites.

ROAD SIGNS

In the early days of the car, street signals were haphazard, usually painted on wood by the local municipality. Over time, they have become standardized and are now typically constructed of 0.08"- to 0.125"-thick sheet aluminum with an applied reflective layer and silk-screened graphics. Engineer-grade signs are coated with two layers of vinyl, one tinted to the color of the sign, and one clear, embedded with a lattice of reflective glass beads. The vinyl content, and difficulty in stripping off the graphics, makes road signs hard to recycle, despite the high value of a big sheet of aluminum.

Sign Salvage

Road signs are all around us, but tampering with them is illegal. To acquire signs legally, call or e-mail the local transportation authorities and ask for any surplus, damaged, bent, or discarded signs. Government and university surplus auctions, typically held once a quarter, are other potential sources. Also check auto junkers, car pick-a-part yards, scrap dealers, flea markets, and, as a last resort, the Internet. New and used signs can be affordable to buy, but shipping can be pricey.

Sheet aluminum is a wonderful material: strong, flexible, and corrosion-proof. Aluminum itself is soft to drill and cut through, and sharp edges can be knocked down with ordinary sandpaper. Use a 40-tooth, carbide-finishing blade to cut straight lines with a circular saw, and a jigsaw with a fine-toothed, metal-cutting blade for precision work. Sheet aluminum can be very difficult to bend due to its ductility (see Bending Sheets on page 152).

STEEL SIGNS

Before plastic and vinyl became the low-cost materials of choice, commercial signs were painted on wood and thin sheet metal. Old signage was used to mend buildings, shoring up garage walls and sections of roof. A sharp-eyed scavenger can find such remnants all over the city, some free for the taking. Look for old signs in all the usual places — flea markets, scrap yards, alleys, and auto-repair shops. Stay away from antique stores, where they are usually being sold as decorations and priced accordingly.

Steel signs (and sheet steel generally) have great tensile strength but are brittle and prone to cracking if fatigued repeatedly. To bend steel, sheets are usually pressed in a brake, a vise-like machine that employs two beveled bars and a lever to crease the steel along a precise edge. The guerilla can just as easily use the edge of a table, hanging the material over and hitting it with a mallet until the desired shape is achieved. Overlapping tabs or flaps can be used to secure bent signs: pin folds in place by through-drilling and bolting or riveting. Steel sheets can be screwed to wood frames to serve as brackets or gussets that lock members in place and prevent racking.

LICENSE PLATES

License plates are churned out by the millions every year. Drivers are supposed to send in their old plates when applying for new tags, but there is little or no penalty for keeping them. Flea markets and vintage stores sell them cheap, a buck or two each, and rare or foreign ones are available on eBay for a bit more.

License plates, like signs, are made of mild sheet steel that is easily bent with a hammer. Bends may zig and zag because the embossed letters and numbers can interfere with proper creasing. Plates can be cut with an angle grinder, rotary tool, or tin snips. Use a flat metal file to knock down any burrs left from cutting or drilling. A few coats of spray metal lacquer will seal in that road-worn patina and make the surface food-safe.

THREADED ROD

Threaded rods, commonly called all-thread, are essentially long, headless bolts. They are available at the hardware store in precut lengths of 1, 2, 3, and 8 feet, in a wide variety of diameters. Threaded along their entire length, the rods often are used in combination with Unistrut (see page 151) to hang ductwork and mechanical equipment. The endless threads make them very adaptable, a sort of plug-and-play Erector set for adults.

Primarily designed (and rated) for hanging applications, all-thread is strongest in tension. When compressed, even beefy ¾" rod will bend. Prevent deflection by running the rod through a pipe, which creates a strong hybrid tensile/compressive structural unit. Threaded rods can be cut with an angle grinder, rotary tool, or hacksaw. Make sure to round off cut edges and bevel the threads, otherwise it will be difficult to get the nuts on later. Another quick way to clean up the threads is to put a nut on either side of the cut line, make the cut, then spin the nuts off over the cut ends, forcing down any burrs.

PIPE

Steel pipe is a hard, thick-walled material used for gas lines and non-drinking water pipes. Black steel is for gas lines, and galvanized is typically used for water lines; their parts are generally interchangeable. The most common diameters are ½", ¾", and 1", each designed to take a different amount of pressure. Much stronger than electrical conduit, steel pipe also comes with threaded ends that accept standardized connectors at various angles. The hard pipe material is heavier, more expensive, and much more difficult to cut than threaded rod and conduit. However, its raw strength and joint standardization make it ideal for knocking together simple, serviceable structural frames.

UNISTRUT

Unistrut, or Superstrut, is heavy-duty steel channel with a pattern of ½"-wide, lozenge-shaped cutouts that accept custom-made fasteners and brackets. It is used to hang ductwork, build mounts for HVAC equipment, and as signposts. The pattern of holes and set of accessories is meant to make a universal kit that can be shaped into any simple right-angled structure. However, as with any kit, its push toward universality results in some limitations. The formed channel makes Unistrut very strong for its weight, and the galvanization makes it weatherproof. Cut with a metal chop saw, an angle grinder, or (laboriously) a hacksaw. The factory-made connectors are expensive and inflexible, so experiment with other hardware-store brackets, bypass framing, or homemade wood joints.

TOOLS

MALLETS

Guerilla metal bending requires the straightforward application of raw strength. Regular hammers are liable to dent, leaving ugly half-moons all over the surface. Use a 3-pound rubber mallet for steel signs and license plates. Aluminum, due to its resiliency, may require a little more horsepower:

Flooring mallets, used for striking flooring nail guns, have a 2-pound cast iron head with a rubber cap. The rubber prevents marring, and the iron lends momentum.

A dead-blow hammer, commonly used in auto work, is another option. Usually molded out of a single piece of polyurethane, the heads are hollow, filled with lead shot or sand to absorb impact and prevent rebounding.

TIN SNIPS

Tin snips are essentially oversize scissors, used for cutting thin sheet metal, guttering, and flashing. They are safe, quiet, and cheap. However, because the blades are offset from one another, they shear when they cut, which can leave an ugly edge. Use a file to clean up any burrs.

POP-RIVET GUN

Rivets are large cylindrical fasteners with a head on one end, designed for joining metal plates. The headless end is then mechanically smashed down, trapping the material. Rivets are used frequently in boats and bridges because they are stronger than bolts in shear applications. In the 1920s, the invention of blind rivets – small aluminum shafts that could be drawn tight from one side – eliminated the need to have access to the back side of the material. Commonly known as pop rivets, they are installed with a simple lever-operated rivet gun (see page 115). Different-sized rivets have different "draws," or maximum thicknesses that they can accommodate.

ANGLE GRINDER

An angle grinder can be fitted with an array of interchangeable discs for working metal:

A cut-off wheel is a thin abrasive blade, used for cutting. Cut-off wheels are fragile and prone to cracking, so be careful not to damage them when setting down the grinder.

Grinding wheels are used for smoothing weld beads and knocking down burrs.

Flap wheels have dozens of tiny flaps of sandpaper, which can be used for rust removal and final polishing. Always wear gloves, earmuffs, and eye protection when using an angle grinder.

METAL CHOP SAW

Metal chop saws operate on the same principle as miter saws (for wood; see page 57), with a few modifications peculiar to the needs of cutting metal. First, the blade is an abrasive disc instead of a toothed wheel. This means the entire surface of the blade is working the cut, instead of just the leading edge. Second, metal chop saws have a clamp in the base to secure material against the fence. Unlike wood, metal is prone to scooting around on the saw base, which can be very dangerous. Metal saws are extremely loud, in an unpleasant, screeching way, throwing large arcs of sparks. Wear gloves, earmuffs, and safety glasses (or, preferably, a full plastic facemask, if available) when using a metal chop saw.

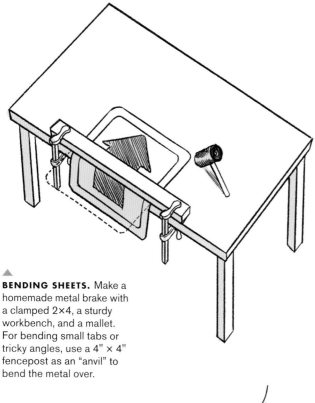

▲
BENDING SHEETS. Make a homemade metal brake with a clamped 2×4, a sturdy workbench, and a mallet. For bending small tabs or tricky angles, use a 4" × 4" fencepost as an "anvil" to bend the metal over.

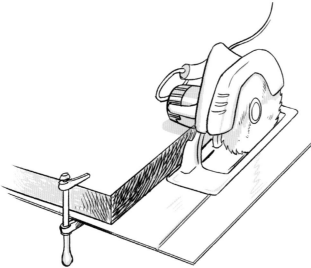

▲
SCORING SIGNS.
To prepare signs for bending, use a clamped straightedge and a circular saw with a carbide blade to score the aluminum no deeper than $1/16$".

METHODS

BENDING SHEETS

Sheet steel, be it signs or license plates, is easy to bend. Hold the material over an edge — a workbench, porch edge, or stair step — and hammer down on the overhanging portion with a mallet. For big pieces or more precise bends, create a homemade brake by clamping a 2×4 aligned with the table edge or other supporting surface, trapping the material between the two sharp edges. Sheet steel is prone to fatigue, and if the bend is worked too much, the metal will weaken and snap. So go slowly and try not to bend back after committing to one direction.

Road signs are much harder to bend, due to the resiliency of the aluminum. The sheet has to be weakened along the eventual folds before the material will crease. One method is simple but time-consuming: Place the metal on a sacrificial wood surface and drill a series of ⅜" holes on 1" centers along the desired fold lines. Be careful to let the drill rest and cool off periodically, as drilling dozens of holes with a relatively big bit can overwhelm the motor. Lay the fold line along the workbench edge and hammer down the overhanging portion until the desired fold angle is achieved. After bending, file the holes to remove any burrs.

Another method involves scoring the aluminum with a circular saw and a carbide-toothed finishing blade. This is a delicate operation, as the signs are so thin it is easy to cut right through them by accident. Set the blade depth to $\frac{1}{16}$" or perhaps a little less. Test-cut into a piece of wood or scrap of aluminum to make sure the blade is not set too deep. Mark the fold lines and run the scores. Go slowly, as the slippery aluminum and shallow cut make the saw prone to wandering. If possible, clamp down a straightedge to run the saw against for maximum accuracy. Flip over the sign, align the score with the work surface edge, and hammer out the fold. Always bend *into* the score, closing the cut; bending *away* from the score will open up the cut and snap the sheet.

BENDING TUBES

Metal conduit is thin-walled and easy to bend. Professional electricians use conduit benders, which have a long arm and a grooved rocker, creating smooth, continuous, kink-free bends. Angle markings along the rocker allow for precise measuring.

Without a bender, the guerilla can make use of a few blocks of wood and some elbow grease: Screw one block of scrap down to a sacrificial surface (the "brace" block). Cut a second block (the "miter" block) to the angle of the desired bend, then screw it down parallel to the brace block, leaving a gap between them as wide as the conduit. The beginning of the miter should align with the end of the brace block. Mark the conduit where you want the bend and lay it between the blocks, aligning that mark with the ends of the miter block and the brace block. Pull until the conduit kinks, gives way, and conforms to the desired angle (see page 156).

NO-WELD JOINERY

Metal is typically a high-heat material — cast, forged, and welded. These methods make for seamless, strong joints but are too costly and specialized for the guerilla. Plates, such as road signs, can be joined with pop rivets: Drill a hole through both pieces and insert the fat, short end of the rivet. Insert the long, skinny end into the rivet gun and pump the handle until the rivet draws tight and snaps off.

Alternatively, if you have access to the back side of the material, use #10 machine bolts with washers on both sides. Pop rivets are typically aluminum, and the soft metal and thin shaft can make them vulnerable to shearing in half if the two plates slide past one another. Machine bolts are much stronger, making them ideal for pinning the folds in chairs.

CONDUIT COATRACK

In tight spaces, hooks are always a good storage solution. Coats, hats, scarves, bike helmets, purses, all corralled and up off the floor. However, many apartment buildings don't allow tenants to put anything in the walls — assuming you could find a solid stud anyway.

The Conduit Coatrack is a minimalist solution, made from bent (super-cheap) electrical conduit. Slim and sturdy, it takes up little space in the apartment or the moving truck, a dependable companion for the winter nomad.

MATERIALS

- Two scraps of 2×4, approximately 12" long
- One scrap of ¾" plywood, approximately 12" by 12"
- 3" drywall screws or clamps
- Three 1¼" #6 wood screws (Spax)
- Three 60" lengths of ¾"-diameter electrical conduit
- Six rubber cane or crutch tips
- 22-gauge copper craft wire, approximately 10 feet

TOOLS

- Pencil
- Tape measure
- Protractor
- Miter saw
- Jigsaw
- Scrap of 100-grit sandpaper
- Speed Square
- Drill/driver
- ⅛" pilot bit
- ¾" spade bit
- Needle-nose pliers

STEPS

1 **Cut a piece of 2×4** with a 30-degree miter. Screw or clamp it down to the floor, workbench, or a half-sheet of scrap plywood. Screw down a second piece of 2×4, perpendicular to the first, with a ¾" gap between the tip of the miter and the edge of the 2×4, as shown below.

2 **Mark each length of conduit** 16" from one end and 8" from the other end. Align one mark with the tip of the miter in the bending jig and pull the conduit until it kinks and conforms to the miter. Flip the piece end-for-end and repeat at the other mark, taking care to keep the two bends in the same plane.

3 **Lay a piece of the conduit** on its "back," so the two bends are pointing upward. About 1" up from the kink in the base bend (16" end) drill a ⅛" hole straight down all the way through the conduit. Repeat for other two pieces of conduit.

4 **Insert a rubber cane tip** into each open end of each piece of conduit.

5 **Using the protractor,** lay out an equilateral triangle with 4" sides in the middle of the plywood scrap (each angle is 60 degrees). Make a mark ¾" from each point (vertex), marking along each side of the triangle (six marks total). Connect the pair of marks near each point, then mark the center of that line. Drill a ¾" hole at each center marking.

6 **Cut out the triangle** with the jigsaw, connecting the three ¾" holes. Ease the edges of the cutout plywood plate with sandpaper.

7 **Nestle a piece of the conduit** into one of the ¾" semicircles of the plywood plate. Screw through the conduit and into the plywood with a #6 wood screw. Taking care not to flex the screw joint too much, rotate the assembly and repeat until all three uprights are fixed to the plywood plate.

8 **Set the rack upright,** with the 16" bent ends forming feet and the 8" bent ends forming hooks. Squeeze the top ends together and lash in place with the copper wire.

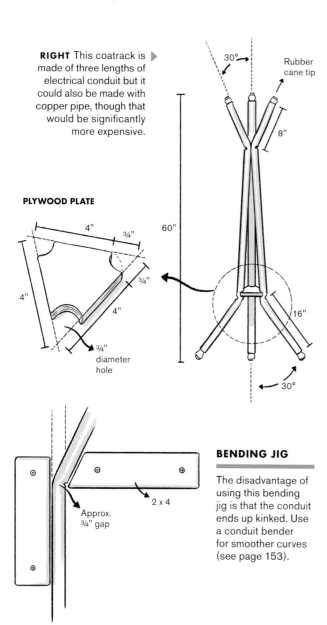

RIGHT This coatrack is made of three lengths of electrical conduit but it could also be made with copper pipe, though that would be significantly more expensive.

PLYWOOD PLATE

BENDING JIG

The disadvantage of using this bending jig is that the conduit ends up kinked. Use a conduit bender for smoother curves (see page 153).

DISPOSAL *Cut the wire, unscrew the plywood triangle, and recycle the uprights.*

LICENSE PLATE BOWL

License plates get a lot of abuse, plowing through slush in the winter and blizzards of insects in summer. After all that hard work, they usually end up forgotten, recycled at the DMV.

The License Plate Bowl preserves the memory of all those road trips, right on the kitchen counter. A set of simple folds forms the plates into a rigid shell, elevated on some bolt feet and sealed with lacquer. The same bending geometry can also be used to make bowls out of road signs. Note that some states require motorists to surrender old plates in order to get new ones. Check with your local DMV, or go guerilla and report them lost.

MATERIALS

- Two license plates
- Seven #10 × ¾" machine bolts or ¼" pop rivets
- Fourteen #10 washers
- Seven #10 nuts
- Four ⅜" × 2½" carriage bolts
- Eight ⅜" cut washers
- Eight ⅜" nuts
- Clear metal spray lacquer

TOOLS

- Sandpaper, 220-grit
- Pencil
- Tape measure
- Square
- Straightedge
- Drill/driver and ⅜" bit
- Adjustable wrenches
- Tin snips
- Needle-nose pliers
- Mallet
- Metal file
- Locking pliers

STEPS

1 **Remove any rust** from the plates with sand-paper and wash with hot soapy water.

2 **Bolt (or rivet) the two plates together** along their long edges, using the old mounting holes. Drill a hole and add a third bolt equidistant between the other two.

3 **Measure 2½" in from each edge** and draw a line on each side, forming a smaller rectangle within the perimeter of the plates, as shown below. In each corner, where the lines cross, drill a ⅜" hole.

4 **Make a diagonal cut** in each corner, connecting the ⅜" hole and the corner of the plate at a 45-degree angle.

5 **Use the needle-nose pliers** to bend up each corner tab along the pencil line, as shown at right.

6 **Lay the plates face-down** on the corner of a workbench, aligning the lines on the plates with the edge of the surface. Pound each of the four sides downward with a mallet, one at a time, using the edge of the table to make a sharp crease. Hit the plates firmly, but go slowly to prevent cracking the brittle steel.

7 **In each corner,** force the tabs to overlap and clamp them together with locking pliers. Drill a hole in the center of the tabs and bolt (or pop-rivet) them together, securing the fold and the bowl shape. Trim off excess tab material to round off corners neatly.

8 **Redrill the corner holes** with a ⅜" bit. Make feet with the ⅜" carriage bolts, sandwiching the plates tightly between two washers and two nuts. Set the bowl upright and adjust the feet with a mallet until they all hit the table evenly.

9 **Wash the bowl again thoroughly,** then seal with several coats of metal lacquer so the bowl is food-safe.

DISPOSAL *Disassemble, reuse the fasteners, and recycle the plates.*

BOWL ASSEMBLY

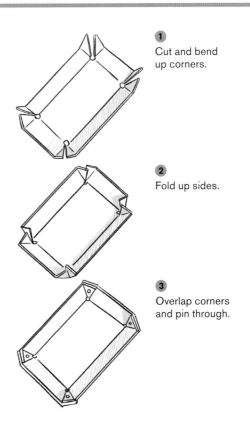

1 Cut and bend up corners.

2 Fold up sides.

3 Overlap corners and pin through.

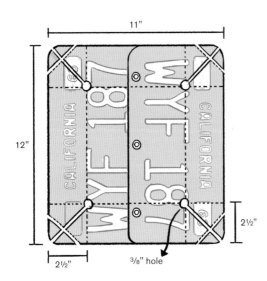

11"

12"

2½"

2½"

⅜" hole

CLAMP TABLE

Simplicity, oft cited as a design ideal, is frustratingly difficult to realize. All furniture runs into certain structural realities, limiting the amount of practical subtraction.

The Clamp Table is the simplest of all guerilla furniture: it uses no fasteners, just physics, and it packs flat in seconds. As weight is applied, each metal frame only clamps down tighter, gaining strength. When on the move, discard the boards and take only the frames; forage fresh planks once you've arrived at your destination.

MATERIALS
- Two 10-foot lengths of Unistrut
- Twelve ¼" × 1" hex-head bolts
- Twelve ¼" nuts
- Twenty-four ¼" fender washers
- Two 48" 2×6s
- One 48" 2×4

TOOLS
- Tape measure
- Permanent marker
- Square
- Angle grinder with metal cut-off blade or metal chop saw
- Metal file
- Locking pliers
- Ratchet set

STEPS

1 **Cut the Unistrut** into ten 18" lengths, taking care to make the cuts as square as possible. De-burr cut edges with the grinder and file.

2 **Using the existing holes** and the ¼" bolts, fasten four lengths into an 18" square as shown below. Measure 1¾" down from the bottom of the top piece of Unistrut and bolt a crossbar into place, using a washer on each side. Use a set of locking pliers to hold the nut and wrench down as tightly as possible on the bolt head. The clear space between the crossbar and the top of the structure is critical. If it's too tight, the frames won't cant out and clamp down on the boards; if it's too loose, the frames will cant out too much and the system won't rigidify. A 1⅝" to 1¾" clear space is about perfect for use with standard 1½"-thick dimensional lumber.

3 **To assemble the table,** stand the frames up on the floor, upside down, about 3 feet apart. Slide the two 2×6s and one 2×4 through the slot in each frame. With a helper, flip the table over. Press down in the middle of the boards until the frames tilt inward and lock into place.

4 **The structure will still have some flex** and a tendency to rock side-to-side. To secure, tap shims or small wood wedges between the top bar of Unistrut and the boards (see photo on page 161).

DISPOSAL *Disassemble and reuse the bolts. Recycle the Unistrut.*

LEG ELEVATIONS

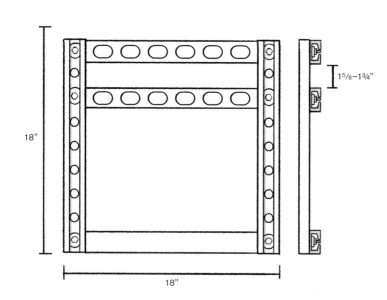

18"

1⅝–1¾"

18"

FORCE DIAGRAM

As force is applied, the bottoms of the frames slide outward, clamping the tops down tighter on the boards.

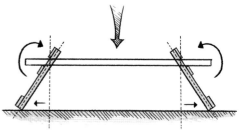

TIP The clamp table could also be made with pipe or square tube stock. The structural system, while sturdy enough to bear considerable weight, will still be susceptible to some lateral flexibility.

CONDUIT LAMP

Like water, light assumes the shape of its container. Most modern fixtures leave light flabby and shapeless, using a piece of plastic to scatter it all over the room. But sometimes, especially late at night, all you need is a slim line of light to read by.

The Conduit Lamp opens a slit in a piece of conduit, bends down three legs, and puts in a small bulb to make a compact bedside lamp. The cylinder emits a thin blade of light, easy to aim for nighttime reading. Dead simple, it uses one material — aluminum — and requires no fasteners, diffuser, or complex wiring.

MATERIALS

- One piece 2"-diameter × 14" aluminum electrical conduit
- Two scraps ¾" plywood, 2" × 12"
- Drywall or wood screws
- One 4"-diameter studio lamp with aluminum shade
- Electrical tape
- One small-diameter CFL or LED bulb, 40W equivalent

TOOLS

- Tape measure
- Cloth measuring tape
- Permanent marker
- Sheet of printer/ notebook paper
- Adjustable square
- Drill/driver
- Two bar clamps
- Angle grinder
- Sandpaper, 100-grit and 220-grit
- Metal file
- Hammer
- Heavy-duty scissors

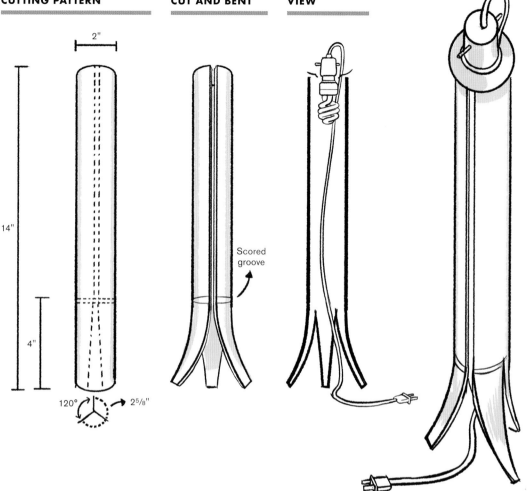

CUTTING PATTERN

2"

14"

4"

120° 2⅝"

CUT AND BENT

Scored groove

SIDE CUTAWAY VIEW

 TIP The conduit lamp could also be made with thin-walled chain-link fence pipe.

STEPS

1 **Make a mark 4" up** from one end of the piece of conduit. Wrap a sheet of paper tightly around the pipe so it forms a straight, continuous edge that's aligned on the mark. Trace along the paper's edge to create a ring around the pipe. Use the angle grinder to lightly score along the line without cutting all the way through the wall of the pipe.

2 **Make a mark on the scored ring.** Using a flexible measuring tape, measure 2⅝" around the scored ring and make a second mark. Repeat to end up with three marks, all equidistant from one another around the circumference of the pipe. Use the square to draw lines at those marks down to the end of the pipe, forming three centerlines. Measure 1" to either side of each centerline, and then connect those points with the top of the centerlines, forming three triangles.

3 **Screw a plywood strip** down to your workbench. Lay the piece of conduit tight against it, then screw down the other strip, trapping the conduit and keeping it from rolling. Clamp

SOCKET-SHADE ASSEMBLY

Aluminum studio clamp lights are available at any hardware store for a few bucks. They can be adapted into new fixtures with little modification, saving the trouble of wiring a lamp from scratch.

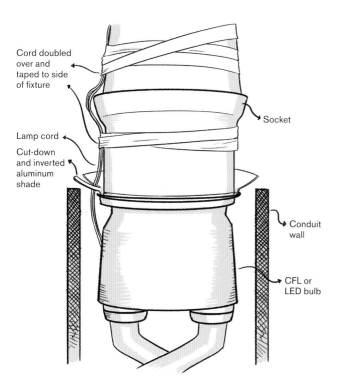

Cord doubled over and taped to side of fixture

Socket

Lamp cord

Cut-down and inverted aluminum shade

Conduit wall

CFL or LED bulb

down the conduit with the two bar clamps. Use the grinder to score along the lines marking the triangles, gradually deepening the grooves until they are cut through.

4   **Draw a straight line** that connects the vertex of one triangle cutout with the opposite end of the pipe, using the adjustable square and registering it against the opposite end of the pipe. Cut along this line, scoring it repeatedly until it cuts through. The slit should be about ¼" to ⅜" wide and as straight as possible. It can be a tricky cut to make; ensure the pipe is tightly clamped, and go slowly.

5   **Clamp the pipe** with the score line made in step 1 against the edge of the workbench and hammer down on each foot until it flares outward.

6   **De-burr all the cuts** with 100-grit sandpaper and a file. Once clean and smooth, polish the body of the pipe with 220-grit sandpaper, then wash with warm soapy water.

7   **Remove the shade** from the studio lamp (see step 4 of Cube Lamp on page 33). Cut it down with scissors until it is a small cone, 2¼" in diameter. Cut a slit in the side to feed the cord back through. Screw it back onto the socket backwards.

8   **Wrap the cord** back against the socket, feeding it through the slit in the shade and taping it to the socket base with electrical tape. Screw in the bulb. Set the assembly into the top of the conduit, feeding the cord through the body of the pipe. Everything should fit very snugly inside.

Note: *Use only a CFL (compact fluorescent) or LED light bulb in this lamp; a standard incandescent bulb creates too much heat and could overheat the aluminum and melt the lamp cord.*

DISPOSAL *Disassemble and recycle the parts.*

WHEELBARROW CHAIR

MATERIALS

- Old steel wheelbarrow
- Spray paint
- 12 feet of 2×4 material
- Wood finish of your choice
- Rags
- Denatured alcohol
- Eight ½" × 2½" hex-head bolts
- Eight ½" nuts
- Sixteen ½" cut washers

TOOLS

- Ratchet
- Crescent wrench
- Wire brush
- Sandpaper, 80-grit (for metal) and finer grits (for wood)
- Pencil
- Tape measure
- Square
- Miter saw (optional)
- Circular saw
- Drill/driver and 1¼" bit
- Clamps
- Angle grinder, rotary tool, or hacksaw

When I worked pouring concrete in Arizona, we made healthy use of wheelbarrows. At break time, we would tip them up on end, handles in the air, and use them as deep bucket seats.

The Wheelbarrow Chair refines this technique into a blue-collar lounge chair, ready for the living room or the back porch. Polish up an old, broken barrow with a wire brush and spray paint, line it with pillows, and put your feet up after a long day.

STEPS

1 **Remove the wheelbarrow bucket** from the handles. Discard handles, hardware, and wheel (saving inner tube for the Inner Tube Stool on page 132). Clean the bucket with a wire brush and 80-grit sandpaper. Brush off the dust, wipe clean with a rag dampened with denatured alcohol, and spray-paint, if desired.

2 **Cut two 2×4 back legs at 32",** mitering the bottom ends at 35 degrees and the top ends at 40 degrees. Cut the two front legs at 42", mitering the bottom ends at 35 degrees and the top ends at 45 degrees. These leg lengths make for a fairly low seat; however, if the center of gravity gets too high on the wheelbarrow it will become very tippy.

3 **Dimensions of wheelbarrows vary,** so space the holes in the legs as far apart as practical, for maximum stability, and center them on the width of the leg. Drill two 1¼"-diameter holes halfway into each leg. These are counterbores for recessing the bolt heads. Complete each hole with a ⅝" bit, drilling all the way through the wood.

4 **Sand and finish each leg** with the finish of your choice.

5 **Clamp the front (longer) legs** to the wheelbarrow bucket, tight to the underside of the lip. The top of the leg should come about three-quarters of the way up the body of the bucket. Adjust the legs until they are aligned with each other. Drill through the holes in the legs and through the bucket. Install the legs with bolts, using washers on both sides. The nuts go on the inside of the bucket; you'll trim off the bolts later.

6 **Clamp the back legs** onto the wheelbarrow so the miters match at the tops of the legs. Drill through the bucket and bolt into place as before.

7 **Trim off any excess bolt length** inside the bucket and line the interior with pillows or cushions to hide the fasteners (see diagram at right).

SIDE ELEVATION

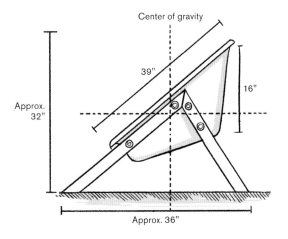

CUT LIST

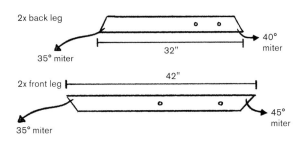

CUSHION SCHEME

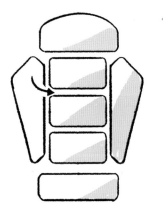

◀ Make a simple set of cushions with scrap fabric, camping sleeping pads (closed-cell foam), and mattress pad foam (open-cell foam). Sew small magnets into the back side of the cushions to secure them to the seat.

DISPOSAL *Remove the legs and burn, compost, or recycle into other projects. Recycle the wheelbarrow bucket at an appropriate facility.*

ROAD SIGN CHAIR

In the sixties, Charles and Ray Eames bent plywood into improbable shapes and mounted the results on elegant wood bases. More recently, a host of designers have done the same in metal and plastic, folding up clever, faceted chair shells and elevating them on geometric legs.

The Road Sign Chair creases, slits, and bends an aluminum road sign into a structural shell. The shell is strong but flexible, making for excellent ergonomics. The sign graphics and sharp wood make for a bright Pop Art living room readymade.

MATERIALS

- One 30"-square road sign
- Scrap plywood
- One 4×4-foot sheet ¾" plywood
- Four 1" #8 machine bolts
- Ten #8 nuts
- Twenty #8 washers
- Wood glue
- 1½" #6 trim-head wood screws
- Twelve #8 rubber washers
- Six 2" #8 machine bolts
- Wood finish of your choice

TOOLS

- Pencil
- Tape measure
- Square
- Straightedge
- Clamps
- Circular saw with 60-tooth carbide finishing blade
- Jigsaw with wood- and metal-cutting blades
- Drill/driver and ¼", ⅜", and ¾" bits
- Mallet
- Locking pliers
- Sandpaper, 100-grit

TIP With minor modifications, the Road Sign Chair could be turned into a side chair or rocking chair. Since the seat and base are structurally independent, you could mount the chair shell to a wide variety of bases.

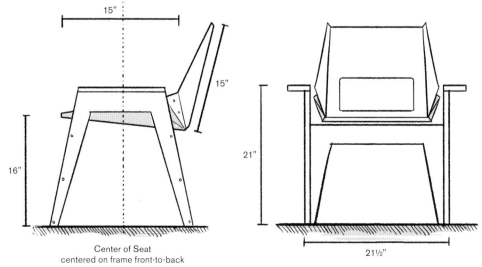

15"

15"

16"

Center of Seat
centered on frame front-to-back

21"

21½"

STEPS

1 On the plain side of the sign, lay out the lines as shown at right. The dashed lines represent *scores* – shallow cuts that do not go all the way through the sign. The double solid lines represent cuts that go all the way through.

2 Lay a sacrificial scrap of plywood over your work surface, and clamp down the sign atop the plywood. Set the blade depth of the circular saw to cut slightly deeper than the thickness of the sign, then make all the marked cuts. As an optional embellishment you can cut out a small rectangle in the small of the back area: Drill a ⅜" hole in each corner of the marked cutout, insert a jigsaw blade, and connect the dots with straight cuts.

3 For the scores, set the circular saw blade to a very shallow depth, about ¹⁄₁₆", and test this depth on a sign scrap. It is critical that these cuts not go more than halfway through the depth of the material, or the sign will be fatally weakened. Use the saw to make the scores (see pages 152-153). Since the blade is not fully penetrating the material, it will have a tendency to skate around; go slowly, use both hands, and clamp down a straightedge.

4 Drill a ⅜" hole at the intersections of the scored lines, as shown at right, above.

5 Hold the triangular tabs at the corners over the corner of a workbench and *gently* hit them with the mallet until they fold up about 30 degrees. Do the same with the sides.

6 Lay the sign flat on its back, bent sides pointing up in the air. Lay a scrap of 2×4, approximately 13" long, on the scored line at the "equator" of the sign. Push down on the 2×4 with one hand while using the other hand to pull the top half of the sign toward your body, bending the sign into an L shape.

7 Clamp together the overlapping triangular tabs in the corners, using locking pliers, a C-clamp,

Make sure the road sign is securely clamped or screwed down before cutting. Freshly cut aluminum will be very sharp; ease edges with some 100-grit sandpaper.

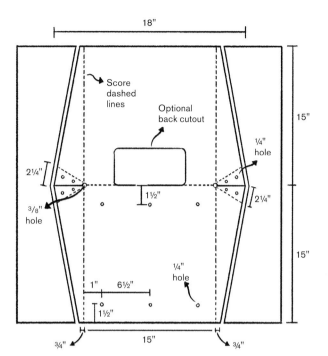

or a small bar clamp. Drill ¼" holes through both overlapping pieces and secure each joint with two 1" machine bolts to complete the chair shell.

8 The chair frame is essentially four U-shaped plywood pieces arranged in a square. Mark the plywood as shown on the next page and make the cuts with the circular saw, finishing the interior corners with a jigsaw. Additionally, cut two strips of plywood at 2¼" × 20" and two at 2¼" × 11½".

9 Spread a thin bead of glue on the edge of one of the 20" plywood strips and clamp to the face of piece "A," aligned with the top edge. Predrill and fasten with trim-head wood screws, making sure the edges stay flush. Scrape up any glue squeeze-out with a putty knife. Repeat with the other 24" strip and piece "C." The sign shell will be fastened to these strips.

Ⓐ FRONT LEGS (CUT 1)

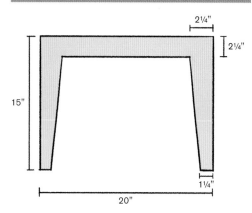

2¼"

2¼"

15"

1¼"

20"

Ⓒ BACK LEGS (CUT 1)

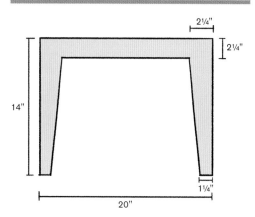

2¼"

2¼"

14"

1¼"

20"

TIP With so few components and simple butt joints, this frame can be adapted to a wide variety of chair designs.

Armrests: 11½" x 2¼"

Road sign mounting strips: 2¼" x 20"

Ⓑ SIDE LEGS (CUT 2)

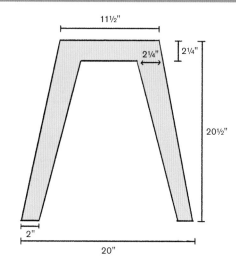

11½"

2¼"

2¼"

20½"

2"

20"

10 **Spread a thin bead of glue** on the outside edge of piece "A" and join to one of the "B" pieces. Predrill and screw together, making sure the edges stay flush. Use three screws per side, evenly spaced for a neat appearance. Repeat for the other side, fastening the second "B" piece. Fasten in piece "C" in the same manner, completing the box.

11 **Glue and screw the 11½" strips of plywood** to the top of each "B" piece, flush to the inside, to make arms.

12 **Sand the frame** and finish as desired.

13 **Position the road sign shell** into the frame, square and centered. The shell should over-

hang the frame a little bit at both the front and back, favoring the front so that the chair doesn't tip when you lean back. Clamp the shell in place. At the front and the back, drill three ¼" holes down through the sign and the plywood strips underneath. Secure the seat to the frame through these holes with the 2" machine bolts, spacing the seat off the frame with the rubber washers, putting two washers around each bolt between the plywood and the seat. Trim off excess bolt length with an angle grinder.

DISPOSAL *Remove the shell from the frame and recycle the shell, if possible. Throw out the frame or fit it with a new seat.*

RECOMMENDED READING

Bouroullec, Ronan and Erwan. *Ronan & Erwan Bouroullec.* **Phaidon Press, 2003.** This definitive monograph on the brothers Bouroullec illustrates the early years of two of today's best furniture designers.

Brand, Stewart, ed. *Whole Earth Catalog.* **1968–2001.** The Internet for hippies and DIYers, before the Internet existed.

Crawford, Matthew B. *Shop Class as Soulcraft: An Inquiry into the Value of Work.* **Penguin, 2009.** A modern philosophical treatise on the value of working with one's hands, written by a man who owns a doctorate in philosophy and a motorcycle repair shop.

Dean, Andrea Oppenheimer. *Proceed and Be Bold: Rural Studio After Samuel Mockbee.* **Princeton Architectural Press, 2005.** The Rural Studio has grown up after a more experimental early period, producing a mature body of work still grounded in a commitment to place, human dignity, and farmyard ingenuity.

Department of the Army. *Survival: Field Manual 21-76.* **Department of the Army, 1970.** All you need to know to survive anywhere in the wild, anywhere in the world, with nothing but a knife and your wits.

Dreyfuss, Henry. *Designing for People,* **3rd ed. Allworth Press, 2003.** A bible for industrial designers, explaining human factors, visual coherence, and a great many other variables in the science of design.

Henry Dreyfuss Associates. *The Measure of Man & Woman,* **rev. ed. John Wiley, 2002.** The original, book-length study of human factors, updated with modern data.

Hennessey, James, and Victor Papanek. *Nomadic Furniture.* **2 vols. Pantheon, 1973 and 1974.** The godfathers of guerilla design outline furniture projects in paper, cardboard, and wood for the apartment-dwelling nomad.

Isaacs, Ken. *How to Build Your Own Living Structures.* **Harmony Books, 1974.** A design philosophy/how-to book illustrating Issacs's modular, reconfigurable designs for furniture and small structures, based on bypass framing and off-the-shelf parts.

Jencks, Charles, and Nathan Silver. *Adhocism: The Case for Improvisation,* **rev ed. MIT Press, 2013.** A serious, thorough book about the place of readymades, ad-hoc solutions, and improvised structures in design culture.

PROJECTS BY USE

178

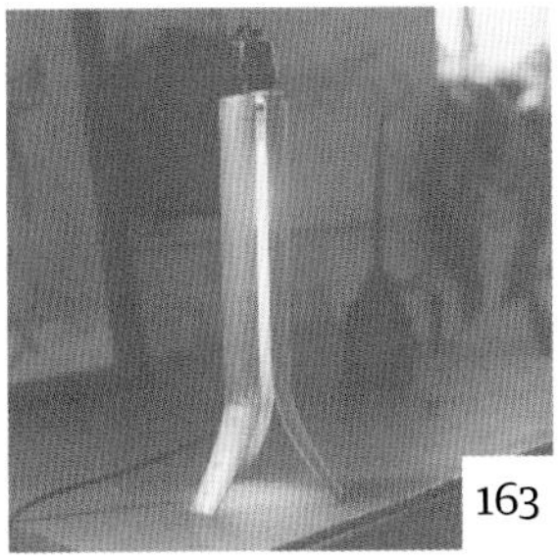
163

TABLES & DESKS

34

74

78

86

94

99

160

ORGANIZATION

64

82

125

139

154

MISC.

38

67

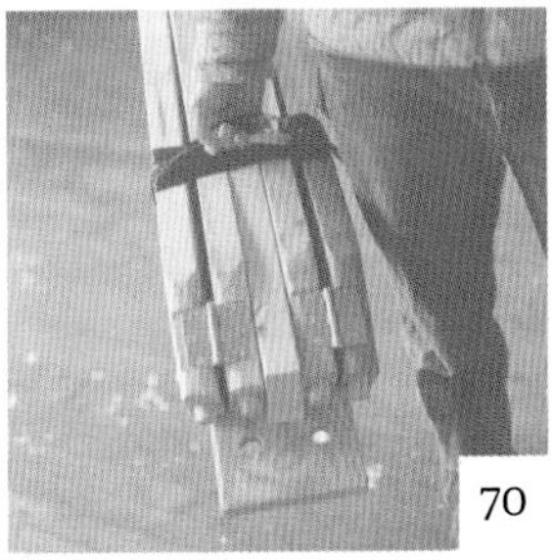
70

157

INDEX

Page numbers in *italic* indicate illustrations or photos; page numbers in **bold** indicate charts.

EXPLORE THE MAKER'S LIFE
WITH THESE OTHER STOREY TITLES

The Good Life Lab
by Wendy Jehanara Tremayne

This is the inspirational story of how one couple ditched their careers and high-pressure life in New York City to move to New Mexico, where they made, built, invented, foraged, and grew all they needed to live self-sufficiently. Alongside their personal story are tips and tutorials as Tremayne teaches you the art of making biofuel, appliances, structures, food, and medicine. Contemplative and action-oriented, *The Good Life Lab* is the manual for life in a postconsumer age.

320 pages. Paper. ISBN 978-1-61212-101-7.

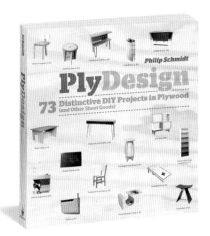

PlyDesign by Philip Schmidt

These 73 ideas for sleek, smart home furnishings can be made from off-the-shelf sheet materials using only basic hand and power tools. With innovative designs contributed by more than 50 creative builders, the projects include tables, stools, workstations, benches, shelves, organizers, headboards, doghouses, and more. A photo of each finished project is accompanied by a list of needed tools and materials, cutting and assembly diagrams, and clear step-by-step instructions.

320 pages. Paper. ISBN 978-1-60342-725-8.

These and other books from Storey Publishing are available wherever quality books are sold or by calling 1-800-441-5700. Visit us at www.storey.com or sign up for our newsletter at www.storey.com/signup.